THE FEDERAL WRITERS' PROJECT
A Bibliography

by
JEUTONNE P. BREWER

The Scarecrow Press, Inc.
Metuchen, N.J., & London
1994

British Library Cataloguing-in-Publication data available

Library of Congress Cataloging-in-Publication Data

Brewer, Jeutonne, 1939–
    The federal writers' project : a bibliography / by Jeutonne P. Brewer.
      p.   cm.
    Includes index.
    ISBN 0-8108-2924-X (alk. paper)
    . 1. Federal Writers' Project—Bibliography. I. Title.
Z1247.B74   1994
[E175.4]   94-18246
016.8108'03273'09043—dc20

In memory of
William L. Patten, who always encouraged me to learn all I could and then teased me about being in school so long,

Clarence E. Brewer, who enjoyed telling stories about the WPA and many other things, and

Anna Mae Sturgeon, who shared many stories about the life and times of early settlers in Oklahoma.

Dedicated to
Ila May Patten for her love and patience, and

Ruth Holbrook Brewer for teaching me the importance of living each day fully.

Table of Contents

A Chronology of the Works Progress Administration

6 May 1935—President Franklin Delano Roosevelt's Executive Order No. 7034 that created the WPA.

July 1935—Federal directors for the arts project appointed. Henry Alsberg appointed director of the Federal Writers' Project.

27 July 1935—"Official birthday" of the Federal Writers' Project [Mangione, *The Dream and the Deal*, p. 29].

2 August 1935—First official announcement of Federal Project No. 1, widely known as "Federal One."

Spring 1936—Sterling A. Brown appointed editor of Negro affairs.

25 June 1936-23 October 1937—John A. Lomax served as national advisor on folklore.

1937—First guides published—Idaho, Washington, DC, and the New England states.

1937-1938—Most of the ex-slave narrative interviews collected.

April 1938—Martin W. Royse appointed consultant on labor and social groups; directed work in Social-Ethnic Studies.

2 May 1938-31 July 1938—Benjamin A. Botkin served as folklore consultant to Federal Writers' Project.

1 August 1938-31 August 1939—Benjamin A. Botkin served as folklore editor of the Federal Writers' Project.

1 September 1939—Works Progress Administration changed to Work Projects Administration. Federal Writers' Project known

as WPA Writers' Program. Projects conducted under state sponsorship.

1941—Last guide published—Oklahoma.

30 June 1943—End of the WPA.

Introduction

President Franklin Delano Roosevelt created the Works Progress Administration when he issued Executive Order No. 7034 on May 6, 1935. He set up a three-part design for central control and service for the white-collar work programs—(1) the Division of Applications and Information, (2) the Advisory Committee on Allotment, and (3) the Works Progress Administration. The WPA, as it came to be called, was the successor to the programs of the Federal Emergency Relief Act.

Harry Hopkins was appointed as administrator of the WPA. In July, 1935, he appointed federal directors for the arts programs—Nikolai Sokoloff for the Music Projects, Holger Cahill for the Art Projects, Henry Alsberg for the Writers' Projects, and Hallie Flanagan for the Theater Projects. The Historical Records Survey, directed by Luther Evans, was part of the Federal Writers' Project until 1936, when the program was moved to the Research and Records Program.

In this way began an innovative and controversial program in which the government supported white-collar and professional programs as well as manual labor and construction programs. The federal government "supported and subsidized an arts program that in material size and cultural character was unprecedented in the history of this or any other nation" (McDonald 1969: ix). Federal Project No. 1, often called "Federal One," was set up to provide cultural programs as part of the general effort to provide jóbs through work relief. Musicians, artists, actors, and writers could apply to work with arts and cultural programs.

The WPA existed for eight years, from July 1, 1935 to June 30, 1943. During that time it provided employment for 8,500,000 individuals, that is, for "nearly one-fourth of all families in the United States..." ("Letter of Transmittal," by George H. Field in the *Final Report on The WPA Program, 1935-43*, p. iii). The largest number of people employed at one time was 3,000,000.

As the list of WPA programs at the end of this section shows, the Federal Writers' Project, was one fairly small segment of this large work relief program. It was not a large program in terms of the number of individuals employed; about 7,000 individuals worked for the program during its existence. Yet, "the least publicized of the three art projects, [the Federal Writers' Project] may emerge as the most influential and valuable of them all" (Cantwell 1939: 325). The reason for this high praise was the best known publications of the Federal Writers' Project—the American Guide books. As many reviewers noted, no guide was perfect; essays within the volumes were typically uneven in quality. However, these publications presented America to Americans with both its beauty spots and its warts. As one reviewer noted, "The material...is amazingly rich and colorful, presented rather informally in a pleasing and always adequate manner. Not one of the books is dull..." (Putnam 1938: 696). The guides showed that the American landscape was colorful and worth seeing, that the culture of America deserved a closer look and a higher degree of appreciation, and that writers with a wide range of talent could work together to produce useful and interesting material. "The America that is beginning to emerge from the books of the Writers' Project is a land to be take seriously: nothing quite like it has ever appeared in our literature" (Cantwell 1939: 323). Even today, the Federal Writers' Project is best known for these state guides.

More material was collected for the state guides than could be used in those volumes. Using that material and collecting more, the Federal Writers' Project also produced city guides and guides to areas of interest, some well known like Death Valley, others less well known like Mt. Tamalpais in Marin County, California. The Federal Writers' Project also provided support for some writers to work on their own, and collected and published volumes of folklore, life-histories of workers and immigrants, and interviews with ex-slaves. Benjamin Botkin noted that these materials would be valuable to scholars studying language and literature.

Yet the end of the WPA programs was barely noticed in 1943. The work of the Federal Writers' Project as well as other WPA programs was largely forgotten. Nearly 20 years passed after the end of World War II before scholars began to look carefully at the WPA and its programs. Perhaps everyone had been eager to forget the years of grinding poverty and despair. Certainly the declaration of war in December, 1941, shifted the focus of this country's leaders and changed the work efforts of its citizens. The work produced by the WPA and its programs was put aside and largely forgotten. After that war, people wanted to put their lives back in order. Jobs were available. No one wanted to bring up a painful past of economic depression. The post-war boom was much more pleasant to participate in and to think about. The beginning of the Cold War, the Korean War, and the period of McCarthyism occupied America's attention in the 1950s. When scholars began to re-evaluate the New Deal, the WPA programs were important to understanding the policies, successes, and failures of the New Deal.

In addition to these major social upheavals, there were other reasons for the individual and the family not to recall the WPA. The public did not understand the complex structure of and the many diverse programs of the WPA. Newspapers regularly criticized the WPA. They did not typically explain the purpose and accomplishments of the programs. Working for the WPA carried a stigma with it. For example, when John Cheever finished his work on the New York City Guide, "he resigned, still feeling uneasy about the disgrace he had brought on his family" (Mangione 1972: 103). If writers did refer to the WPA in their fiction, the comment was typically like that of Wilhelm in Saul Bellow's *Seize the Day*: "The WPA ditch had brought the family into contempt" (New York: Viking Press, 1961 [1956], p. 38).

> Among some members of the Writers' Project 'WPA' connoted a stigma of the lowest order, a dark and embarrassing symbol of a time of their lives when circumstances beyond their control compelled them to admit on public record, personal defeat. For some the memory of their experience on the [Writers'] Project, no matter how fruitful it had been, became a secret shame, something that, if possible, should be concealed. It is a pathetic commentary on the ramifications of human insecurity that only a few of the writers who successfully nurtured their young literary talents on the Writers' Project ever made any mention of it in their published autobiographical statements. (Mangione 1972: 119)

The depression was not forgotten, however. Children born in the 1930s, 1940s, and 1950s are children of the Great Depression, not because they lived through it but because their parents or grandparents did. These hard times changed their lives, affected the way they looked at the world. These children grew up hearing stories about the depression and jokes about the "boondogglers" who leaned on their WPA shovels.

I remember those stories about struggle and survival. Later, I came to realize that although people talked about their memories of the Great War, the depression, World War II, about how they grew survival gardens or Victory gardens, how they survived during the depression, or what "war work" they did, they never talked about working for the WPA. Also, I do not remember the WPA and its contributions rating more than perhaps a mention in history or literature classes. I learned about the work of the WPA through books and by chance rather than through family stories or classes in school.

This bibliography really began while I was writing my dissertation, a study of the language of ex-slaves as reflected in the ex-slave narratives collected by the Federal Writers' Project in the late 1930s. As I continued my research after completing my graduate degree, I collected and filed references, notes, and ideas. Like all research, each article, book, and citation about the WPA led to information about the broad scope of the WPA—ex-slave narratives, life-histories, ethnic studies, poster project, the Living Newspaper, "boondoggling," and construction of schools and highways. When I began to review and reorganize this large collection of quotes and notes on slips of paper, I began to organize a bibliography of the WPA.

The primary purpose of this volume is to provide a working bibliography that will make information about the Federal Writers' Project more accessible to researchers by listing the major sources. The primary focus of this volume is the Federal Writers' Project, although it includes a few items about the Historical Records Survey and the Federal Theater Project if they relate to the work and organization of the Federal Writers' Project. Section 1 lists works about the Federal Writers' Project. I include items (1) that discuss, explain the work, policies and publications of the Federal Writers' Project; (2) that evaluate the work of the FWP, including retrospective comments and recent calls for the revival of WPA-type programs; (3) that discuss or explain connections of the FWP with other WPA projects; and (4) that explain WPA policies and activities that had an effect on the success or failure of WPA programs at the national, state, or local levels. Criteria 3 and 4 are the most general. Criterion 3, for example, includes items that refer to interconnections between the Historical Records Survey and the FWP. Criterion 4 includes items like Roger Biles's book *Memphis in the Great Depression*, which explains briefly that projects for artists and writers foundered because of traditional Southern attitudes toward "make work" programs.

Section 2 lists works produced by the Federal Writers' Project. With few exceptions, I list only works that have been published. For example, it seemed appropriate to list some of the mimeographed literary magazines that Project writers produced. I have included the state, city, and local guides by state. "Local" here means location of a particular tourist area usually identified with a state. For example, publications about Death Valley are listed as part of the California publications, information about the Berkshire Hills is listed with the Massachusetts publications. Regional publications include entries about tourist highways, the intracoastal waterway, and the Oregon Trail. The section, "Other Publications," includes publications that are about ethnic groups, life-stories, pioneer tales and tall tales, and such topics of general interest as how our government functions, bibliographies, indexes, and animals and plants. The final part of this section contains an extensive, although not exhaustive, list of Federal Writers' Project writers. The list includes primarily writers who worked on the American Guides.

Every research project grows out of past research and owes a debt to other researchers. The bibliography of Arthur Scharf, published as an appendix in Jerre Mangione's *The Dream and the Deal*, has been an important source for anyone with an interest in the Federal Writers' Project. *Government and the Arts in Thirties America*, edited by Roy Rosenzweig et al., provides a listing of materials in the National Archives, the primary repository for the Federal Writers' Project as well as other WPA arts projects. This bibliography includes a section on works about the Federal Writers' Project as well as a section on works by the Federal Writers' Project, extensive annotations, and a list of writers who worked with the Federal Writers' Project.

Like all research projects, this one has limitations and probably some gaps. With few exceptions like the guide to Washington, DC, the Federal Writers' Project publications were published by regional and local as well as national publishers. Finding and listing all the items of a publishing venture spread among many publishers—large and small, nationally known and relatively unknown—requires searches through standard references and tracking down chance, often brief mention of items. I welcome additions and corrections. The items in the bibliography have been entered into a computer listing, so that I can continue to add to them.

While working on this bibliography, I have received aid and encouragement from many people. Chris Brewer has patiently lived through another research project with his quiet humor; I deeply appreciate his continuing support. As research assistants, Donald Jenkins, Mark Caskie, and David Schwartz spent many hours in the library, checking and double-checking details about references; Sheldon Pacotti helped with proofreading the manuscript. Marlene Pratto, director of Instructional and Research Computing, patiently answered my many questions about using the computer. I thank her for her time, patience, and encouragement. I appreciate the time that Boyd Davis of the University of North Carolina at Charlotte gave to our many discussions about the project, even when I interrupted our collaborative research projects to talk about the Federal Writers' Project. Cindy Bernstein of Auburn University, Greta Little of the University of South Carolina, and Natalie Maynor of Mississippi State University provided words of encouragement during the past few years when it seemed that this project might have to be delayed one more time. I enjoyed discussing the WPA with my colleague, SallyAnn Ferguson, who appreciates the significance of the ex-slave narratives collected by the Federal Writers' Project. I thank James Evans, the Head of the English department, for his interest in my research and his understanding of complex but important connections between different disciplines. It is a pleasure to work with Jim, who provides enlightened leadership with a touch of humor.

Organization of the Works Progress Administration

Engineering and Construction
Municipal Engineering Projects
Airport and Airway Projects
Public Building Projects
Highway and Road Projects
Conservation Projects
Engineering Survey Projects
Disaster Emergency Activities

Service
Public Activities
  Adult Education
  Nursery Schools
  Library Services
  Recreation Projects
  Federal Project No. 1
    Music Projects
    Art Projects
    Writers' Projects
      Creative Work
      American Guide
      Folklore Studies
      Slave Narratives
      Social-Ethnic Studies
      Negro Studies
    Theater Projects
  Research and Records
    Research
      Social and Economic Surveys and Studies
      Research Assistance Projects
    Records
      Public Records Projects
      Historical Records Survey
  Welfare Projects
    Sewing Projects
    Other Goods Projects
    School Lunch Projects
    Gardening and Canning Projects
    Housekeeping Aide Projects
    Surplus Commodity Distribution Projects
    Public Health Projects

Hospital Aide Projects
Other Welfare Projects [shoe repairing, matron service for schools, cleaning and renovating buildings, toy-lending libraries, and legal aid]

Safety Program
Supply Methods and Property Administration
Division of Investigation
Defense and War Activities
Training and Reemployment
Training Program for WPA Foremen
Household Workers' Training
Vocational Training Under the Adult Education Program
Training for Defense and War Work
Vocational Training School Projects
In-Plant Preemployment Training
Auxiliary Shop Training
Women Train for Defense and War Work
Training Physically Handicapped Persons
Airport Servicemen Training
Training for Nonprofessional Work in Hospitals

[List based on the *Final Report on the WPA Program, 1935-43*, by U.S. Federal Works Agency (Washington, DC: Superintendent of Documents, U.S. Government Printing Office, 1943) and *Federal Relief Administration and the Arts*, by William F. McDonald (Columbus, OH: Ohio State University Press, 1969).]

Section 1

Works about the Federal Writers' Project

1   Aaron, Daniel. "Guide-Books and Meal Tickets." *Times Literary Supplement,* 28 July 1978, p. 837.

       Review of *The Federal Writers' Project,* by Monty Noam Penkower.

2   Aaron, Daniel. "Thirty Years Later: Memories of the First American Writers' Congress." *American Scholar* 35 (Summer 1935): 495-516.

       Kenneth Burke, Malcolm Cowley, Granville Hicks, and William Phillips discussed the First Writers' Congress, its contribution to "a new war between literary generations," its influence on the founding of the League of American Writers, and the views of writers at the time of the meeting. Includes comments about Phillips' work with Dwight Macdonald, Mary McCarthy, Eleanor Clark, and Fred Dupee to disrupt the Second Writers' Congress.

3   Aaron, Daniel. "The Treachery of Recollection." *Carleton Miscellany* 6 (Summer 1965): 3-126.

       "Until a short time ago, scholars and writers rather studiedly avoided the Thirties." The post World War II "new literary stance was conservative, formal, and non-committal" with little good to say "for the popular Left-wing writers of the Thirties or for the literary forms and styles these writers had used...." The essay deals generally with the problems of understanding and writing about the ideas and literature of the Thirties. Although not limited to FWP writers, the general points are useful and informative.

4   Aaron, Daniel. *Writers on the Left: Episodes in American Literary Communism.* New York, NY: Harcourt, Brace and World, 1961. 460 pp.

5   Aaron, Daniel and Robert Bendiner, eds. *The Strenuous Decade: A Social and Intellectual Record of the 1930's*. Documents in American Civilization Series. Garden City, NY: Anchor Books, 1970. 537 pp.

6   Adams, Grace K. "The White Collar Chokes: Three Years of WPA Professional Work." *Harpers Magazine* (October 1938): 474-484.

7   Adams, Grace [Kinkle]. *Workers on Relief*. New Haven, CT: Yale University Press, 1939. 344 pp.

8   Agnew, Brad. "Voices From the Land Run of 1889." *Chronicles of Oklahoma* 67 (1989): 4-29.
         Discusses the social and legal aspects of the land rush, based on transcripts in the Indian-Pioneer History collection of the Oklahoma Historical Society.

9   "Alfred Smith Dies; Labor Official Aided Black Government Workers." *Washington Post*, 29 May 1986, Section C, p. 6.
         Reports that Alfred E. Smith began his career in federal government with the WPA in the 1930s, where he tried to have the WPA writers and arts projects hire blacks.

10   Alsberg, Henry G. "Federal Writers' Project and Education." *Journal of the National Education Association* 25 (March 1936): 86.

11   Alsberg, Henry. Speech at the Second Congress of American Writers. In Henry Hart, ed., *The Writer in a Changing World*. New York, NY: Equinox Cooperative Press, 1937.

12   Alsberg, Henry G. "Writers and the Government: A Letter from the Director of the Federal Writers' Project." *Saturday Review of Literature*, 4 January 1936, pp. 9, 23.
         "The project of The American Guide was inaugurated in order to solve the problem of caring for writers who need government aid and who at the same time must preserve their integrity and independence." Claims that the work is interesting to writers for the information and insight they gain, while the thirty hours of work leaves them enough time and energy to use "their talents for outside work." Lists Harry Kemp, John Moroso, Ross Santee, and Edward Dahlberg as well-known writers employed by the project.

13   Antone, Joe and Nellie Coombs. "We Work on the WPA: Captain Joe Antone, Cape Verdean Seaman." *Spinner: People and Culture in Southeastern Massachusetts* 4 (1988): 125-131.

Presents an edited transcript of two interviews conducted with Captain Joe Antone, who was a whaler on a New Bedford, Massachusetts, schooner.

14 Appel, Benjamin. *The People Talk.* New York, NY: E.P. Dutton and Company, Inc., 1940.

15 Atchison, Sandra. "A Trip Through the Past with the WPA." *Business Week,* 22 October 1990, p. 122.

Discusses the value of the state Guides as "collectibles" as they are being rediscovered by "a new generation of readers and travelers."

16 Badger, Anthony J. *The New Deal: The Depression Years, 1933-1940.* American Century Series. New York, NY: Noonday Press, 1989. 392 pp.

17 Bailey, Guy and Marvin Bassett. "Invariant *BE* in the Lower South." In *Language Variety in the South: Perspectives in Black and White,* pp. 158-179, edited by Michael B. Montgomery and Guy Bailey. University, AL: University of Alabama Press, 1986.

Analyzes the use of unconjugated or invariant *be* in the data provided by the Linguistic Atlas of the Gulf States. Compares the findings with those of language use in northern urban cities, in Atlanta, in the ex-slave narratives collected by the Federal Writers' Project.

18 Bailey, Guy and Natalie Maynor. "The Present Tense of *be* in Southern Black Folk Speech." *American Speech* 60 (1985): 195-213.

19 Balch, J[ack] S. *Lamps at High Noon.* New York, NY: Modern Age Books, 1941.

A novel that deals with working on the Federal Writers' Project.

20 Banks, Ann, ed. *First Person America.* New York, NY: Alfred A. Knopf, 1980. Distributed by Random House. 287 pp.

Includes eighty narratives from the Federal Writers' Project, a collection of stories told by granite workers, textile workers, circus and rodeo and con-game people, and ex-slaves. Banks discusses Botkin's work with the FWP, the goals of the project, and some of the individuals who worked for the Federal Writers' Project, for example, Ralph Ellison, Margaret Walker, Zora Neale Hurston, Arna Bontemps, Richard Yerby, Richard Wright, Nelson Algren, Jack Conroy, May

Swenson, Saul Bellow, John Cheever, and Conrad Aiken. "Of the forty-one Federal Writers whose work appears in this book, more than half published books after they left the Project."

21   Banks, Ann. "Making It Through Hard Times." *Atlantic* (July 1980), p. 40-44, 49-57.

22   Banks, Ann. "Tobacco Talk." *Southern Exposure* 8:4 (1980): 34-45.

      Describes stories about tobacco farming in the 1930s. The stories were collected as part of the work of the Federal Writers' Project.

23   Banks, Ann and Robert Carter. *Survey of Federal Writers' Project Manuscript Holdings in State Depositories.* Foreword by Alan Brinkley. Washington, DC: American History Association, 1985. 32 pp.

24   Barnes, Peter. "Bringing Back the WPA." *New Republic*, 15 March 1975, p. 19-21.

25   Barrese, Edward. *American Archivist* 44 (Spring 1981): 161.

      Review of *The WPA Historical Records Survey: A Guide to the Unpublished Inventories, Indexes and Transcripts.* [Chicago, IL: Society of American Archivists, 1980. 42 pp.]

26   Barrese, Edward Francis. "The Historical Records Survey: A Nation Acts To Save Its Memory." Ph.D. dissertation, George Washington University, 1980.

      Luther Evans, the director of the Historical Records Survey, managed to separate the program from the Federal Writers' Project in 1936, "when it became clear that the Survey resources were being allocated for Writers' Project programs." The HRS produced nearly two thousand research aids and played an important part in promoting an "archival awakening," including the "foundation of the National Archives."

27   Batchen, Lou Sage. "La Curandera." *El Palacio* 81:1 (Spring 1975): 20-25.

28   Batchen, Lou Sage. "Festivals." *El Palacio* 81:1 (Spring 1975): 26-30.

      Includes excerpts from the WPA archives about festivals in New Mexico, including Las Posadas, La Noche Buena, Los Dias, St. John's Day, and Farmer's Patron Day.

29   Bauman, John F. and Thomas H. Coode. *In the Eye of the Great Depression: New Deal Reporters and the Agony of the Ameri-*

can People. DeKalb, IL: Northern Illinois University Press, 1988. 230 pp.

Discusses the reports of sixteen reporters sent by Harry Hopkins to investigate and evaluate the conditions of the unemployed and the efforts of local relief agencies. Reports sent to Hopkins reflect both the miserable conditions throughout the country and the views and attitudes of the reporters.

30   Bell, Clive. "Art in the Planned State." *Forum* 97 (May 1937): 306-309.

31   Bendiner, Robert. *Just Around the Corner: A Highly Selective History of the Thirties*. New York, NY: Harper and Row, 1967.
Reprinted New York, NY: E. P. Dutton, 1968, 268 pp. paper.

32   Bendiner, Robert. "Thirties: When Culture Came to Main Street." *Saturday Review*, 1 April 1967, p. 19-21.

Notes first that the New Deal, unlike most depression era governments, provided free piano lessons for housewives, free marionnette shows as well as the works of Christopher Marlowe, and produced "volumes of first rate Americana." Lists Conrad Aiken, John Cheever, Richard Wright, Maxwell Bodenheim, George W. Cronyn, Edward Dahlberg, John Steinbeck, Vardis Fisher, Vincent McHugh, Claude McKay, and Harry Kemp as "memorable names" connected with the Writers' Project. "It was, all in all, a magnificent experiment."

33   Benét, Stephen Vincent. "Patchwork Quilt of These United States." New York Herald-Tribune *Books*, 28 December 1941, p. 1.

34   Bergen, John V. "The US 67 Corridor in the WPA's Illinois Tour Guide." *Western Illinois Regional Studies* 14:1 (1991): 49-68.
Explores the rural and town descriptions published in the state guide published in 1939 by the Federal Writers' Project.

35   Berry, Mary Frances and John W. Blassingame. *Long Memory: The Black Experience in America*. New York, NY: Oxford University Press, 1982. 486 pp.

36   Biddle, George. "The Government and the Arts." *Harper's* (October 1943): 427-434.

37   Biles, Roger. *Memphis in the Great Depression*. 1st ed. Knoxville, TN: University of Tennessee Press, 1986. 174 pp.
Explains briefly that projects for artists and writers foundered because of traditional Southern attitudes toward "make work" programs. Claims that the New Deal worked through the local

political machine rather than trying to change it with the result that Memphis remained "the domain of a shockingly autocratic political machine, and the guardian of a rigid racial caste system."

38   Billington, Monroe. "Black Slavery in Indian Territory: The Ex-Slave Narratives." *Chronicles of Oklahoma,* 60:1 (1982): 56-65.

Discusses the former slaves' statements about slave occupations and treatment by Indian masters, as recorded in the interviews collected by the Federal Writers' Project.

39   Billington, Ray Allen "Government and the Arts: The W.P.A. Experience." *American Quarterly* 13 (Winter 1961): 466-471.

Notes that government aid for the arts "began in 1817 when Congress authorized John Trumbull to execute four historic paintings...." The arts programs, including the Federal Writers' Project, "added much to America's cultural wealth" while providing a "case study of the problems involved in government support for the arts." Claims the Federal Writers' Project had a tendency "to stifle the creative genius of many...employees," but reminds critics that the arts projects functioned primarily as relief agencies rather than as programs "intended only to foster culture."

40   Binkley, Robert C. "The Cultural Program of the W.P.A." *Harvard Educational Review* 9 (March 1939): 156-174.

41   Birdsall, Esther K. "The FWP and the Popular Press." In *Challenges in American Culture,* edited by Ray Browne et al. Bowling Green, OH: Bowling Green University Popular Press, 1970.

42   Bishop, Jack. *Ralph Ellison.* Introduction by Coretta Scott King. Black Americans of Achievement Series. New York, NY: Chelsea House, 1988. 112 pp.

Includes comments about Ellison's experience with the Federal Writers' Project. A young adult book for grades 5 and up.

43   Blakey, George T. *Hard Times and New Deal in Kentucky, 1929-1939.* Lexington, KY: University Press of Kentucky, 1986. 252 pp.

44   Blassingame, John W. *The Slave Community: Plantation Life in the Antebellum South.* Revised and enlarged ed. New York, NY: Oxford University Press, 1979. 414 pp.

> Discusses culture, personality types, plantation life, runaways, and the family during slavery from three views—the slave, the planter, and from neutral outsiders.

45   Blassingame, John W., ed. *Slave Testimony: Two Centuries of Letters, Speeches, Interviews, and Autobiographies.* Baton Rouge: Louisiana State University, 1977.

> Provides an unconventional history of American slaves through personal narratives.

46   Blassingame, John W. "Using the Testimony of Ex-Slaves: Approaches and Problems." *Journal of Southern History* 41 (1975): 473-492. Reprinted in *The Slave's Narrative*, pp. 78-97, edited by Paul D. Escott, Charles T. Davis, and Henry Louis Gates, Jr. Oxford, England: Oxford University Press, 1985.

> Claims the antebellum slave narratives are more valuable that the ex-slave narratives collected by workers for the Federal Writers' Project. Studies of the WPA narratives require attention to several problems—being able to recognize the possible bias of the interview situation, working with typescripts that are not necessarily verbatim accounts, taking into account the age of the ex-slaves at the time of the interviews. Claims the antebellum written slave narratives have three advantages over the FWP interviews—writers of the narratives were younger when their stories were collected, were adults when they obtained freedom, and produced longer narratives than the FWP interviews.

47   Blosser, Susan Sokol and Clyde Norman Wilson, Jr. *The Southern Historical Collection: A Guide to Manuscripts.* Chapel Hill, NC: University of North Carolina Library, 1970. n.p.

> Provides a list of papers and description of them with some information about the correspondents. Includes an outline of subjects, for example, the heading, "Negro Slavery," lists papers by state and by category.

48   Bloxom, Marguerite D. *Pickaxe and Pencil: References for the Study of the WPA.* Washington, DC: Library of Congress, 1982. 87 pp.

49   Bluestein, Gene. *The Voice of the Folk: Folklore and American Literary Theory.* Boston, MA: University of Massachusetts Press, 1972. 170 pp.

50   Blumberg, Barbara. *The New Deal and the Unemployed: The View From New York City*. Lewisburg, PA: Bucknell University Press, 1979. 332 pp.

51   Blumberg, Barbara Marilyn. "The Works Progress Administration in New York City: A Case Study of the New Deal in Action." Ph.D. dissertation, Columbia University, 1974.

52   Bogh, Jens and Steffen Skovmand. *Six American Novels: From New Deal to New Frontier*. Aarhus: Akademisk Boghandel, 1972. 337 pp.

53   Bolles, Blair. "The Federal Writers' Project." *Saturday Review of Literature*, 9 July 1938, pp. 3-4, 18-19.

      Claims that John Baker, Assistant WPA Administrator, convinced Harry Hopkins to set up a program for writers and artists, who could "yield something of lasting value for the whole country...." Notes two major problems in setting up the national project: finding state directors and developing a set of instructions for the state directors. Reed Harris and Katherine Kellock served as part of the efficient staff of Henry Alsberg, Director of the Federal Writers' Project. Lists the state directors and notes the accomplishments of FWP writers who received Guggenheim Fellowships, wrote a prize novel, and published their work in a number of magazines. Refers to the work of a number of writers: Miriam Allen de Ford, Vardis Fisher, Lyle Saxon, Jeremiah Digges (Josef Berger), and B. A. Botkin.

54   Bordelon, Pamela G. "The Federal Writers' Project's Mirror to America: The Florida Reflection." Ph.D. dissertation, Louisiana State University and Agricultural and Mechanical College, 1991.

      Stresses the contributions made to American scholarship in cultural studies. Notes that the Federal Writers' Project in Florida "pioneered African-American studies...and revolutionized the study of folklore." Also notes that Zora Neale Hurston worked with the Florida program for a year and a half.

55   Boskin, Joseph. "Sambo: the National Jester in Popular Culture." In *The Great Fear: Race in the Mind of the Americas*, edited by Gary B. Nash and Richard Weiss. Berkshire Studies in American History. New York: Holt, Rinehart and Winston, 1970.

56   Boswell, George W. and Thomas M. Pullen. "Mississippi Folk
      Names of Plants." *Kentucky Folklore Record* 22:3 (July-Oc-
      tober 1976): 64-69.
      From the 1930s to the 1970s, WPA workers and students of
      folk literature collected more than 100 folk names and scien-
      tific names for plants native to Misssissippi.

57   Botkin, B[enjamin]. A. "Applied Folklore: Creating Under-
      standing Through Folklore." *Southern Folklore Quarterly*
      17:3 (September 1953): 199-206.

58   Botkin, Benjamin, ed. *Lay My Burden Down: A Folk History of
      Slavery.* Chicago, IL: University of Chicago Press, 1945. 285
      pp.
      Includes a collection of ex-slave reminiscences culled from
      the WPA slave narratives. Selected on the basis of literary
      quality and general interest, the narratives have been edited
      to remove spelling problems and to change sentence structure
      in order to increase their appeal to the general audience.

59   Botkin, Benjamin A. "Living Lore on the New York City Writ-
      ers' Project." *New York Folklore Quarterly* 2 (November
      1946): 256.

60   Botkin, Benjamin A. "Regionalism: Cult or Culture?" *English
      Journal* 25 (March 1936): 181.

61   Botkin, B. A. "The Slave As His Own Interpreter." *Library of
      Congress Quarterly Journal of Current Acquisitions* 2
      (1944): 37-63.
      Discusses the importance of the slave narratives to the study
      of folklore, language, and literature.

62   Botkin, Benjamin A. Speech at Third Congress of American
      Writers. In Donald Ogden Stewart, ed., *Fighting Words.*
      Third Congress of American Writers. New York, NY: Har-
      court, Brace and Company, 1940.
      Claims the life-history stories collected by the Federal Writ-
      ers' Project were "the stuff of literature."

63   Botkin, Benjamin A. *A Treasury of American Folklore.* New
      York, NY: Crown, 1944. 932 pp.
      Includes selections of Chicago industrial tales by Jack Conroy
      and Nelson Algren.

64   Botkin, Benjamin A. "We Call It 'Living Lore.'" *New York
      Folklore Quarterly* 14 (Autumn 1958): 158.

Describes the folklore work of the Federal Writers' Project "the greatest educational as well as social experiment of our time." Experience with this folklore material could influence a writer's view by providing "a social and cultural consciousness too often lacking in ivory-tower writing."

65   Botkin, Benjamin A. "WPA and Folklore Research: 'Bread' and 'Song'." *Southern Folklore Quarterly* 3:1 (March 1939): 7-14. Reprinted as an appendix in *Conservation of Culture: Folklorists and the Public Sector*, edited by Burt Feintuch.

Notes the close relationship of 'bread' and 'song' in folklore and relates that to the WPA which stressed "the relation between art and life, between work and culture." Explains the integration and cooperation of programs in the second part of the article which was originally a paper presented at the 1938 meeting of the Modern Language Association.

66   Boynton, Maria. *Journal of American Folklore* 97 (April-June 1984): 237-238.

Review of *Up Before Daylight: Life Histories from the Alabama Writers' Project, 1938-1939*, by James Seay Brown. [University, AL: University of Alabama Press, 1982. 261 pp.]

67   Braeman, John. *American Studies* 16 (Fall 1975): 97-98.

Review of *Roosevelt's Image Brokers: Poets, Playwrights and the Use of the Lincoln Symbol*, by Alfred Haworth Jones. [Port Washington, NY: Kennikat Press, 1974.]

68   Braeman, John, Robert H. Bremner, and David Brody, eds. *The New Deal*. Modern America series. 2 Vols. Columbus, OH: Ohio State University Press, 1975.

Discusses the effects of national policies on such areas as fiction, the legal profession, blacks, and agriculture (Vol. 1) and the programs at the state and local levels (Vol. 2).

69   Brandt, R. P. "The Dies Committee: An Appraisal." *Atlantic Monthly* 155 (February 1940): 232.

70   Brasch, Walter M. *Black English and the Mass Media*. Amherst, MA: University of Massachusetts Press, 1981. 345 pp.

Discusses briefly the Federal Writers' Project slave narratives in the context of his cyclical theory of mass media.

71   Brewer, Jeutonne P. "Black English, New Evidence, and Where Do We Go From Here?" *American Speech* 61 (Summer 1986): 153-159.

Review of *Morphologische und syntaktische Variablen im americanischen Early Black English,* by Edgar W. Schneider. [Frankfurt, Germany: Verlag Peter Lang, 1981.]

72   Brewer, Jeutonne P. "Durative Marker or Hypercorrection? The Case of *-s* in the WPA Ex-Slave Narratives." In *Language Variety in the South: Perspectives in Black and White,* edited by Michael B. Montgomery and Guy Bailey, pp. 131-148. University, AL: University of Alabama Press, 1986. 427 pp.

Analyzes the use of the nonconcord verbal *-s* ending as used in the ex-slave narratives collected by the Federal Writers' Project and compares the results with studies of Black English as spoken in northern urban settings and with historical information about British and American dialects.

73   Brewer, Jeutonne P. "Nonagreeing *Am* and Invariant *Be* in Early Black English." *SECOL Bulletin* 3 (1979): 81-100.

Analyzes the use of non-concord *am,* that is, the use of *am* with pronoun subjects other than *I,* and invariant *be* in 31 of the 143 narrative interviews collected by the Federal Writers' Project in South Carolina. Notes that both linguistic forms are "regionally distinct forms."

74   Brewer, Jeutonne P. "Songs, Sermons, and Life-Stories: The Legacy of the Ex-Slave Narratives." In *The Emergence of Black English: Texts and Commentary,* edited by Guy Bailey, Natalie Maynor, and Patricia Cukor-Avila. Amsterdam: John Benjamins.

Focuses on the social and historical context in which the ex-slave interviews of the Federal Writers' Project and disc-recorded interviews of the Archive of Folk Song in the Library of Congress were collected. Combines this material with information provided in interviews with John Henry Faulk, who recorded on disc a significant number of the interviews collected by the Archive of Folk Song. Claims that questions about function of linguistic forms and the origins of Black English "cannot be addressed without the kinds of complementary coverage provided by the WPA narratives and the AFS recordings."

75   Brewer, Jeutonne. "Subject Concord of *be* in Early Black English." *American Speech* 48 (Spring-Summer 1973): 5-21. Reprinted in *Papers in Language Variation,* pp. 161-176, edited by David L. Shores and Carole P. Hines. University, AL: University of Alabama Press, 1977.

Presents the first study of the linguistic characteristics of the
ex-slave interviews collected by the Federal Writers' Project.
Focuses on the uses of the verb *be* in 22 narratives from four
states.

76   Brewer, Jeutonne Patten. "The Verb *Be* in Early Black English:
A Study Based on the WPA Ex-Slave Narratives." Ph.D.
dissertation, University of North Carolina at Chapel Hill,
1974.

Presents a detailed analysis of variation in the use of the verb
be in ex-slave narratives collected by the Federal Writers'
Project. Notes that the grammatical similarities in 40 narratives collected by different interviewers in four different
states provide insight into the process of syntactic change in
early Black English.

77   Brewer, Jeutonne P. 1980. "The WPA Slave Narratives As Linguistic Data." *Orbis* 29 (1980 [1982]): 30-54.

Discusses the ex-slave narratives collected by the Federal
Writers' Project in relation to the procedures for collecting
and editing the materials. Cites examples of and reproduces
copies of state and national correspondence discussing editorial policies. Gives information about John Henry Faulk's
efforts to make disc recordings of interviews with ex-slaves
for the Library of Congress in the early 1940s.

78   Brogan, Dennis. "Inside America." *Spectator*, 28 November
1941, pp. 507-508.

79   Brogan, Dennis. "Uncle Sam's Guides." *Spectator*, 5 August
1938, pp. 226-227.

80   Browder, Nathaniel Clenroy, ed. *Just Plain Folks: In Their Own
Words*. Raleigh, NC: Nathaniel C. Browder, 1983.

Provides abstracts of stories collected by the Federal Writers'
Project.

81   Brown, James Seay, Jr., ed. *Up Before Daylight: Life Histories
from the Alabama Writers' Project, 1938-1939*. University,
AL: University of Alabama Press, 1982. 261 pp.

82   Brown, Lorin W., Charles L. Briggs and Marta Weigle. *Hispano
Folklife of New Mexico: The Lorin W. Brown Federal Writ-
ers' Project Manuscripts*. Albuquerque, NM: University of
New Mexico Press, 1978. 279 pp.

83   Brown, Sterling A. "A Century of Negro Portraiture in American
Literature." *Massachusetts Review* 7 (Winter 1966): 73.

84   Brown, Virginia Pounds and Laurella Owens. *Toting the Lead Row: Ruby Pickens Tartt, Alabama Folklorist.* University, AL: University of Alabama Press, 1981. 180 pp.

85   Burns, John F. "The NHPRC and the State of Washington's Historical Records." *Prologue* 11:1 (Spring 1979): 57-63.

        Notes that the success of current survey projects, supported by the National Historical Publications and Records Commission, are indebted to the work completed by the WPA projects, which provide infomation about where to find records.

86   Burran, James A. "The WPA in Nashville, 1935-1943." *Tennessee Historical Quarterly* 34:3 (Fall 1974): 293-306.

        Discusses the history and administration of the WPA construction and service projects in Nashville, Tennessee, including the 1939 investigation of charges of misuse of money and power in the WPA projects directed by adminstrator Colonel Harry S. Berry.

87   Busby, Mark. *Ralph Ellison.* Twayne's United States Authors Series, No. 582. Boston, MA: Twayne Publishers, 1991. 172 pp.

88   Cade, John B. "Out of the Mouths of Ex-Slaves." *Journal of Negro History* 20:3 (July 1935): 294-337.

        Discusses housing, religion, slave-trading, and slave customs, based on interviews with ex-slaves collected by Cade, a teacher in Louisiana, and his students. Important as a previous study, a model, for the Federal Writers' Project.

89   Cadwallader, D. E. and F. J. Wilson. "Folklore Medicine Among Georgia's Piedmont Negroes After the Civil War." *Georgia Historical Quarterly* 49 (1965): 217-227.

        Presents information about material in the Federal Writers' manuscripts concerning how blacks used plants for medicinal purposes.

90   Campbell, Clarice T. *Journal of Mississippi History* 41 (August 1979): 267-270.

        Review of *The American Slave: A Composite Autobiography*, edited by George P. Rawick, Jan Hillegas, Ken Lawrence. Supplement Series 1, Vol. 6-10, Mississippi Narratives. Contributions in Afro-American and African Studies, no. 35. [Westport, CT: Greenwood, 1977.]

91   Canby, Henry Seidel. *Saturday Review of Literature*, 26 November 1932, p. 270.

A brief, ambiguous statement about the question, "Should Writers Go on a Salary?" of interest in relation to the New Deal programs. States that perhaps literature should have a status like "medicine, where a good doctor is assured of an income, but not of getting rich."

92   Cantor, George. *Where the Old Roads Go: Driving the First Federal Highways of the Northeast.* New York, NY: Harper-Collins, 1990. 320 pp. paper.

Describes old federal highways as a pleasant alternative to travel on the interstates.

93   Cantwell, Robert. "America and the Writers' Project." *New Republic*, 26 April 1939, pp. 323-325. Reprinted in Warren Susman, ed., *Culture and Commitment 1929-1945*, pp. 194-202. New York, NY: George Braziller, 1973.

Claims that the Federal Writers' Project, "the least publicized of the three art projects...may emerge as the most influential and valuable of them all." The state guides and the city guides present American history "in terms of communities...and in terms of the ups and downs of the towns from which the actors emerged and in which the economic movements had their play."

94   Carleton, Anne. *Anne Carleton, 1878-1968: Views of Artists, Beaches, the Depression, Ogunquit, W.P.A. Days in Portsmouth, N.H.* Hingham, MA : Pierce Galleries, Inc., 1982. 10 pp.

95   Carmichael, Dan. UPI Report. Washington News Section. 5 December 1986.

Senator Paul Simon said that "unemployment in America can be cured by an $8 billion government jobs program similar to President Roosevelt's Depression-era Works Progress Administration."

96   Chapman, Maristan. "The Trouble with Authors." *Bookman* 74 (December 1931): 368-370.

97   Chatterton, Wayne. *Vardis Fisher: The Frontier and Regional Works.* Boise State College Western Writers Series, No. 1. Boise, ID: Boise State College, 1972. 51 pp.

98   Chatterton, Wayne and Martha Heasley Cox. *Nelson Algren.* Boston: Twayne Publishers, 1975.

99   Clark, James C. "Klan Buster." *Orlando Sentinel*, 7 July 1991, 3 Star Edition, Florida Section, p. 8.

Includes comments about Stetson Kennedy's work as a "junior interviewer" with the Federal Writers' Project in Florida. Worked with Zora Neale Hurston in collecting interviews.

100   Clark, James C. "1930s Project Recorded Recollections of Slavery." *Orlando Sentinel*, 18 February 1990, Section F, p. 12.

Describes Zora Neale Hurston's work with the Federal Writers' Project to collect interviews from ex-slaves.

101   Clayton, Ronnie W. "Federal Writers' Project for Blacks in Louisiana." *Louisiana History* 19:3 (1978): 327-335.

Discusses a black writers' group formed at Dillard University through the initiative of Lyle Saxon, director of the Louisiana Federal Writers' Project. Notes that the group's project, a Negro history in Louisiana, was never published and that the group's records have disappeared from Dillard University.

102   Clayton, Ronnie W. "A History of the Federal Writers' Project in Louisiana." Ph.D. dissertation, Louisiana State University, 1974.

103   Cobb James C. and Michael V. Namorato, eds. *The New Deal and the South: Essays*. 9th Annual Chancellor's Symposium on Southern History, 1983. Jackson, MS: University Press of Mississippi, 1984. 173 pp.

Includes essays by Frank Freidel, Pete Daniel, J. Wayne Flynt, Alan Brinkley, Harvard Sitkoff, and Numan V. Bartley.

104   Cohen, David S., ed. *America the Dream of My Life: Selections from the Federal Writers' Project's New Jersey Ethnic Survey*. New Brunswick, NJ: Rutgers University Press, 1990. 250 pp.

105   Colby, Merle. "Presenting America to All Americans." *Publishers Weekly*, 3 May 1941, pp. 1828-1831.

106   Cole, John Y. "Amassing American 'Stuff': The Library of Congress and the Federal Arts Projects of the 1930s." *Quarterly Journal of the Library of Congress* 40:4 (1983): 356-389.

The Library of Congress collected the artistic and historical works of such WPA programs as the Federal Writers' Project and the Historical Records Survey, both part of Federal Project Number One.

107   Cole, John Y. "WPA Research Materials at the Library of Congress: A Review and Progress Report." *Library of Congress Information Bulletin*, 29 November 1974, pp. 243-245.

108   Coleman, J[ohn] Winston [Jr.]. *A Bibliography of Kentucky History.* Lexington, KY: University of Kentucky Press, 1949. 516 pp.

109   Coleman, J[ohn] Winston, Jr. *Slavery Times in Kentucky.* Chapel Hill, NC: University of North Carolina Press, 1940. 351 pp.

110   "Collecting Gullah Folklore." *Southern Exposure* 5: 2-3 (Summer-Fall 1977): 119-21.

       Discusses the interviews collected by Genevieve W. Chandler, including techniques for recording interviews collected by hand rather than by machine.

111   "Completion of American Guide Series." *Publishers' Weekly*, 3 May 1941, p. 1815.

112   Congdon, Don, ed. *The Thirties: A Time to Remember.* New York, NY: Simon and Schuster, 1962. 625 pp.

113   Conroy, Jack. "American Stuff: An Anthology of WPA Creative Writing." *New Masses*, 14 September 1937, p. 24.

114   Conroy, Jack. *The Disinherited.* New York, 1933.

       Reprinted with introduction by Daniel Aaron. American Century Series. New York, NY: Hill and Wang, 1963. 310 pp.

115   Conroy, Jack. "Writers Disturbing the Peace." *New Masses*, 17 November 1936, p. 13.

116   Cordes, George P., ed. *WPA: A Philadelphia Retrospective.* Washington, DC: US GSA, 1984. 40 pp.

117   Corlew, Robert E. [Review of *The WPA Guide to Tennessee*]. *Tennessee Historical Quarterly* 46 (Spring 1987): 54-55.

118   Coulter, E. Merton. *The South During Reconstruction: 1865-1877.* A History of the South, Vol. 8. Wendell Holmes Stephenson and E. Merton Coulter, series editors. Baton Rouge, LA: Louisiana State University Press and The Littlefield Fund for Southern History of The University of Texas, 1947. 426 pp.

119   Countryman, Edward. "A World the Slaves Made." *Slavery and Abolition* [Department of Comparative American Studies, University of Warwick, England] 6:2 (September 1985): 160-167.

       Review of *Down by the Riverside: A South Carolina Slave Community* by Charles Joyner [Urbana, IL: University of Illinois Press, 1984. 345 pp].

120   Cowley, Malcolm. "Federal Writers' Project." *New Republic* (October 1972): 23-26.

121   Cowley, Malcolm. "The 1930's Were an Age of Faith." *New York Times Book Review*, 13 December 1964, p. 16.

122   Crawford, Stephen Cooban. "Quantified Memory: A Study of the WPA and Fisk University Slave Narrative Collections." Ph.D. dissertation, University of Chicago, 1980.

Presents a quantitative analysis of the WPA and the Fisk University slave narratives, about 2,000 narratives contained in the original 19 volumes [1972] published by Greenwood. Claims that potential bias based on race of the interviewer is restricted to controversial issues such as punishment and sexual relations. Finds that "punishment was more related to social control than work."

123   Culbert, David H. "The Infinite Variety of Mass Experience: The Great Depression, W.P.A. Interviews, and Student Family History Projects." *Louisiana History*, 19:1 (Winter 1978): 43-63.

Compares the WPA life histories with the family histories written by the author's students at Louisiana State University. Concludes that both provide valuable information about surviving and living in the 1930s.

124   Current-Garcia, E. "American Panorama." *Prairie Schooner* 12 (1938): 79-90.

125   Current-Garcia, E. "Writers in the Sticks." *Prairie Schooner* 12 (Winter 1938): 294-309.

126   Davidson, Katherine H., ed. *Preliminary Inventory of the Records of the Federal Writers' Project, Work Projects Administration, 1935-44.* Washington, DC: National Archives, 1953.

127   Davis, Charles T. and Michel Fabre. *Richard Wright: A Primary Bibliography*. A Reference Publication in Afro-American Studies. Charles T. Davis, Editor. Henry-Louis Gates, Jr., Associate Editor. Boston, MA: G. K. Hall, 1982.

Includes lists for *Daily Worker* articles about WPA activities in 1937 and typescripts for the Federal Writers' Project editorial conference and script for a radio broadcast in essays section for 1938.

128   Davis, Charles T. and Henry Louis Gates, Jr. *The Slave's Narrative*. New York, NY: Oxford University Press, 1985.

Includes one section that focuses on the slave narratives collected by the Federal Writers' Project, the remainder of the book dealing with slave narratives published before 1865.

Claims that the Federal Writers' Project slave narratives are the "oral counterpart" of Vernon Loggins' 1931 study of written texts of slave narratives printed before 1865.

129   Davis, David Brion, ed. *The Fear of Conspiracy: Images of Un-American Subversion from the Revolution to the Present.* Ithaca, NY: Cornell University Press, 1971.

130   Davis, David Brion. "Slavery and the Post-World II Historians." *Daedalus* 103:2 (Spring 1974): 1-16.

Mentions *The Making of the Black Community*, a part of *The American Slave: A Composite Autobiography*, by George Rawick.

131   "Defense Is Not the WPA." Editorial. *Washington Post*, 27 February 1984, Section A, p. 10.

Claims that military spending could have a negative effect on the economy. "Talking about defense as a gigantic WPA project...is worse than misleading."

132   Degler, Carl N. "Freedom After Slavery." *Virginia Quarterly Review* 56 (1980): 345-356.

Review of *Been in the Storm So Long: The Aftermath of Slavery*, by Leon Litwack [New York, NY: Knopf, 1979].

133   Dent, Tom. "Octave Lilly, Jr.: In Memoriam." *The Crisis* 83:7 (1976): 243-244.

Octave Lilly interviewed blacks in New Orleans for the Federal Writers' Project, "a very crucial experience" for Lilly as a young poet. After this period he did not write again until the late 1960s, because he had to "tend to the business of making a living."

134   DeParle, Jason. "Latest Plan to Cure Welfare Troubles Borrows W.P.A. Blueprints of 1930's." *New York Times*, 13 March 1992, Section A, p. 8, 14.

135   DeParle, Jason. "Nostalgia and Need Conjure up Thoughts of the W.P.A." *New York Times*, 3 May 1992, Section 4, p. 6.

136   Derrick, W. Edwin. *Mid-America* 61 (January 1979): 69.

Review of *Roosevelt's Image Brokers: Poets, Playwrights and the Use of the Lincoln Symbol*, by Alfred Haworth Jones [Port Washington, NY: Kennikat Press, 1974].

137   DeVoto, Bernard. "Distributing the WPA Guides." *Publishers Weekly*, 11 May 1940, pp. 1836-1839.

138   DeVoto, Bernard. "The First WPA Guide." *Saturday Review of Literature*, 27 February 1937, p. 8.

139   DeVoto, Bernard. "New England Via WPA." *Saturday Review of Literature*, 14 May 1938, p. 4.

140   DeVoto, Bernard. "The Writers' Project." *Harper's Magazine* (January 1942): 221-224.
      States that the term "Writers' Project is a misnomer...It has been, in fact, a project for research workers." Serving on a committee of writers "asked to make suggestions for the future of the Writers' Project," DeVoto discusses the idea that "the government should conduct the various Projects as a cultural subsidy rather than as relief."

141   Dieterich, Herbert R. "The New Deal Cultural Projects in Wyoming: A Survey and Appraisal." *Annals of Wyoming* 52:2 (1980): 30-44.
      Discusses the contributions of the Federal Arts Project in music, theater, writing, and art, programs for the unemployed that were accepted by Wyoming citizens despite their skepticism toward federal relief programs.

142   Dillard, J. L. *Black English: Its History and Usage in the United States.* New York, NY: Random House, 1972. 361 pp.
      Uses the Federal Writers' Project ex-slave narratives as one of many historical sources to discuss the history and development of black dialects in America.

143   "Distributing the Guides." *Publishers' Weekly*, 11 May 1940, p. 1836.

144   Dobak, William A. "Black Regulars Speak." *Panhandle-Plains History Review* 47 (1974): 19-27.
      Provides accounts of black soldiers based on information in the narratives of the Federal Writers' Project.

145   Donohue, H. E. F. *Conversations with Nelson Algren.* New York, NY: Hill and Wang, 1964. 333 pp.

146   Dorsett, Lyle W. "Frank Hague, Franklin Roosevelt and the Politics of the New Deal." *New Jersey History* 94:1 (Spring 1976): 23-35.
      Discusses the political power of Frank Hague, the mayor of Jersey City, in relation to the WPA programs in New Jersey, programs in which a number of abuses occurred.

147   Doty, C. Stewart. *The First Franco-Americans: New England Life Histories from the Federal Writers' Project 1938-1939.* Orono, ME: University of Maine at Orono Press, 1985. 163 pp.

148   Doty, C. Stewart. "Going to the States: Testimony from the Franco-American Life History Narratives in the Federal Writers Project, 1938-1939." *Contemporary French Civilization* 7:3 (1983): 275-292.

Discusses the experiences of immigrants who came to New England from Quebec and Acadia.

149   Dover, Cedric. "Literary Opportunity in America." *Left Review* 3 (May 1938): 932.

150   Drennen, Marguerite. "New Deal's Huge Cultural Program Launched With $27,000,000 Fund." *Washington Sunday Post,* 8 September 1935.

151   Dubin, Steven C. "Artistic Production and Social Control." *Social Forces* 64:3 (March 1986): 667-688.

Claims that control of production was necessary in the WPA programs because artists and the bureaucracy had little experience in working together. Compares the experiences of artists who worked for the WPA with the experiences of artists who worked for the Comprehensive Employment and Training Act programs in the 1970s and 1980s.

152   Dubin, Steven C. *Bureaucratizing the Muse: Public Funds and the Cultural Worker.* Chicago, IL: University of Chicago Press, 1987. 226 pp.

Contains some comparisons of the WPA projects and the recent CETA arts projects, the "only two large-scale commitments of public support directly to artists within this century." Claims that of the WPA arts projects, the FWP was best able to exercise control of the production, although the example relates only to the state Guide projects.

153   Dubofsky, Melvyn and Stephen Burwood. *Women and Minorities During the Great Depression.* The Great Depression and the New Deal, No. 6. New York, NY: Garland, 1990. 349 pp.

154   Durr, Virginia Foster. *Outside the Magic Circle: The Autobiography of Virginia Foster Durr.* Edited by Hollinger F. Barnard. Foreword by Studs Terkel. University, AL: University of Alabama Press, 1985. 360 pp.

155   Dwyer-Shick, Susan. "The Development of Folklore and Folklife Research in the Federal Writers' Project, 1935-1943." *Keystone Folklore Quarterly* 20 (Fall 1975): 12-14.

156   Dwyer-Shick, Susan. "Review Essay: Folklore and Government Support." *Journal of American Folklore* 89: 354 (October-December 1976): 476-486.

Reviews *Federal Relief Administration and the Arts: The Origins and Administrative History of the Arts Project of the Works Progress Administration,* by William F. McDonald and *The Dream and the Deal: The Federal Writer's Project, 1935-1943,* by Jerre Mangione.

157   Early, Frances. *Canadian Historical Review* 67 (September 1986): 406.

Review of *The First Franco-Americans: New England Life Histories from the Federal Writers' Project 1938-1939,* by C. Stewart Doty. [University of Maine Press, 1985. 163 pp.]

158   Eden, Robert, ed. *The New Deal and Its Legacy: Critique and Reappraisal.* Contributions in American History, No. 132. Jon L. Wakelyn, series editor. New York, NY: Greenwood Press, 1989. 263 pp.

159   Egypt, Ophelia Settle, J. Masuoka, and Charles S. Johnson, eds. *Unwritten History of Slavery.* Social Science Source Documents No. 1. Nashville, TN: Social Science Institute, Fisk University, 1945.

Reprinted Washington, DC: NCR/Microcard Press, 1968.

Also included as part of Rawick 1972.

160   Eisen, Jack. "Alphabet City." *Washington Post,* 1 February 1986, Section: B, p. 2.

NRA may typically mean the National Rifle Association today, but in the time of the New Deal 1930s NRA mean the National Recovery Act; ADA referred to the Alley Dwelling Authority. "One had to live through that era to appreciate the jokes about President Franklin Delano Roosevelt's 'alphabet agencies'," for example, the NRA, WPA, PWA, TVA, CCC, and NLRB.

161   Erickson, Herman. "WPA Strike and Trials of 1939." *Minnesota History* 42 (1971): 203-214.

Examines the causes of a nationwide strike by about 100,000 WPA workers when the Federal Relief Administration Act reduced hourly wages for WPA workers. Notes that national attention focused on workers in Minneapolis and St. Paul, where the strike started, because of violence between workers and police.

162   Erickson, Herman. *WPA Strike and Trials of 1939.* Institute of Labor and Industrial Relations, Reprint Series No. 218. Reprinted from *Minnesota History,* Summer 1971. Urbana, IL: University of Illinois Press, 1971. 214 pp.

163   Escott, Paul D. "The Art and Science of Reading WPA Slave
        Narratives." In *The Slave's Narrative*, pp. 40-48, edited by
        Paul D. Escott, Charles T. Davis, and Henry Louis Gates, Jr.
        Oxford, England: Oxford University Press, 1985. 342 pp.

        Claims that both quantitative and qualitative methods are
        important in studying the slave narratives collected by the
        Federal Writers' Project. Notes that quantitative methods help
        scholars check their impressions, confirm the "validity of
        conclusions," and check "impressions when the matters at
        issue concern perceptions."

164   Escott, Paul D. "The Context of Freedom: Georgia's Slaves
        During the Civil War." *Georgia Historical Quarterly* 58:1
        (1974): 79-104.

165   Escott, Paul D. *Slavery Remembered: A Record of Twentieth-
        Century Slave Narratives*. Chapel Hill, NC: University of
        North Carolina Press, 1979.

        An important source for quantitative and qualitative analysis
        of the ex-slave narratives collected by the Federal Writers'
        Project. Received the 1979 Mayflower Cup award for North
        Carolina nonfiction.

166   Escott, Paul D. "Speaking of Slavery: The Historical Value of the
        Recording with Former Slaves." In *The Emergence of Black
        English: Text and Commentary*, pp. 123-132, edited by Guy
        Bailey, Natalie Maynor, and Patricia Cukor-Avila. Amster-
        dam: John Benjamins, 1991.

        States that the ex-slave narratives collected by the Federal
        Writers' Project "had assumed a central role in the rewriting
        of the history of slavery." Notes that the disc-recorded inter-
        views "suggest what was clear" in the FWP narratives about
        attitudes toward masters and slave whipping and provide
        "direct evidence of the...dynamics of the interview."

167   Evans, Timothy K. "This Certainly Is Relief: Matthew S. Murray
        and Missouri Politics During the Depression." *Bulletin of the
        Missouri Historical Society* 28 (1972): 219-233.

        Examines the rise and fall of Murray, who was the adminis-
        trator for the WPA in Missouri. Explains that Murray devel-
        oped within the WPA a political organization like that he
        developed in Kansas City as part of the Democratic political
        machine of Tom Pendergrast.

168   Evett, Kenneth. "Back to WPA," in column titled, "Kenneth Evett
        on Art." *New Republic*, 24 November 1973, p. 21-22.

169   Faris, David E. "Narrative Form and Oral History: Some Prob-
      lems and Possibilities." *International Journal of Oral History*
      1:3 (November 1980): 159-180.

      Discusses a narrative collected by the Federal Writers' Project
      in relation to the study of oral history as narrative and con-
      ventions of style. See articles by Tom Terrill and Jerrold
      Hirsch and by Leonard Rapport for discussion and contro-
      versy about the narrative.

170   Farran, Don. "Federal Writers' Number." *New Masses*, 10 May
      1938, pp. 97-127.

171   Farran, Don. "The Federals in Iowa: A Hawkeye Guidebook in
      the Making." *Annals of Iowa* (Winter 1973): 1190-1196.

172   Fasold, Ralph. "One Hundred Years from Syntax to Phonology."
      In *Diachronic Syntax*, edited by Sanford B. Steever, Carole
      A. Walker, and Salikoko S. Mufwene, pp. 79-87. Chicago,
      IL: Chicago Linguistic Society, 1976.

      Presents steps in the decreolization of the copula and zero
      copula forms in Black English dialects, based on the Federal
      Writers' Project ex-slave narratives published in Benjamin
      Botkin's *Lay My Burden Down*.

173   "Federal Guide Disturbs Massachusetts Officials." *Publishers'
      Weekly*, 28 August 1937, p. 713.

174   "Federal Poets: An Anthology." *New Republic*, 11 May 1938,
      pp. 10-12.

      "This brief anthology of poets connected with the Federal
      Writers' Project was selected and edited with the help of Sol
      Funaroff." Includes poems by Maxwell Bodenheim, Sterling
      A. Brown, Kenneth Fearing, Eli Siegel, Kenneth Rexroth, and
      Helen Neville.

175   Filler, Louis. *The Anxious Years: America in the 1930s, A Col-
      lection of Contemporary Writings*. New York, NY: Putnam,
      1963.

176   Fisher, Vardis. *Orphans in Gethsemane: A Novel of the Past in
      the Present*. Denver, CO: Alan Swallow, 1960.

      A novel that deals with working on the Federal Writers'
      Project.

177   Fleming, Douglas L. "The New Deal in Atlanta: A Review of the
      Major Programs." *Atlanta Historical Journal* 30 (1986): 23-
      45.

178   Flora, Joseph M. *Vardis Fisher*. New Haven, CT: College and
        University Press, by special arrangement with Twayne Pub-
        lishers, 1965. 158 pp.

        Contains a brief reference to Vardis Fisher's work as the
        director of the Federal Writers' Project of the WPA in Idaho.
        Recognizes Fisher's extensive contribution to Idaho's FWP
        publications. Notes that "Fisher finally resigned because of
        his disgust over the incompetence and waste by project offi-
        cials."

179   Flynt, Wayne. *Georgia Historical Quarterly* 67 (Summer 1983):
        274-276.

        Review of *Up before Daylight: Life Histories from the Ala-
        bama Writers' Project, 1938-1939*, by James Seay Brown.
        [University, AL: University of Alabama Press, 1982. 261 pp.]

180   *Folders of Illinois Folklore in WPA Collections in the Archive of
        Folk Song*. Washington, DC: Library of Congress, Archive of
        Folk Song 1981. 3 pp.

181   *Folklore and Related Activities of the WPA in the Collections of
        the Archive of Folk Song: A Fact Sheet*. Washington, DC: The
        Archive, 1980. 2 pp.

182   Fox, Daniel M. "The Achievement of the Federal Writers' Pro-
        ject." *American Quarterly* 13:1 (Spring 1961): 3-19.

183   Franklin, John Hope. *From Slavery to Freedom: A History of
        American Negroes*. New York, NY: Alfred A. Knopf, 1947.
        Reprint New York, NY: Alfred A. Knopf, 1967.

        This work covers African American history from slavery to
        the mid 1960s. Includes an extensive bibliography.

184   Frisch, Michael. "Oral History and Hard Times." *Oral History
        Review* (1979): 70-79. Reprinted from *Red Buffalo: A Journal
        of American Studies* 1:2-3 (1972): 217-231.

        An article about the different types of reviews of *Hard Times*,
        by Studs Terkel. Notes two assumptions about the functions
        of oral history: "a source of historical information and in-
        sights" or "a way of bypassing historical interpretation."
        Concludes that "failure forced people to reduce general expe-
        riences to personal terms" while "survival...seems to encour-
        age them to elevate personal and biographical generalization
        into historical terms."

185   Fry, Gladys-Marie. *Night Riders in Black Folk History*.
        Knoxville, TN: The University of Tennessee Press, 1975.
        251 pp.

Uses the ex-slave narratives as source material to discuss the KKK and other control-by-fear groups from before and after emancipation. She talks about the effect of the Klan and other groups on the blacks, and about the Night Doctors in Washington, D.C., patrol groups.

186 Gannett, Lewis. "Reading About America." *Publishers' Weekly,* 3 May 1941, pp. 1818-1819.

187 Genovese, Eugene D. "Getting to Know the Slaves." *New York Review of Books,* 21 September 1972, pp. 16-19.

188 Genovese, Eugene D. *Roll, Jordan, Roll.* New York: Pantheon Books, 1974. 825 pp.

Claims that the slaves had lives and minds of their own and that they were not docile creatures who submitted to whipping. Uses the slave narratives collected by the Federal Writers' Project as a major source of information.

189 *Georgia Materials From the WPA in the Archive of Folk Song.* Washington, DC: The Archive, 1981. 4 pp.

190 Gilliam, Dorothy. "Debate on the Underclass." *Washington Post,* 10 July 1986, Section C, p. 3.

Discusses Nicholas Lemann's claim that there is a "strong correlation between underclass status in the North and a family background in the nascent underclass of the sharecropper South." In his *Atlantic Monthly* articles, Lemann viewed the ghetto problem as primarily a cultural problem; therefore, he advocated bringing back the federal WPA.

191 Glassman, Steve and Kathryn Lee Seidel, eds. *Zora in Florida.* University Presses of Central Florida, 1991. 197 pp.

Includes a collection of 15 essays that are "the first in which anyone seriously examines the contribution of Florida material to Hurston's work...." according to the introduction. Notes the imprtance of her work with the Federal Writers' Project in Florida.

192 Glicksberg, Charles I. "Reading About America." *South Atlantic Quarterly* 37 (April 1938): 157-169.

Notes that the federal government, recognizing that "unemployment was a collective problem which must be solved on a national scale," made a "sound and fruitful investment" in the Federal Writers' Project, which has become something more "vital" than a relief project: "has demonstrated that the government can effectively promote cultural and creative activities," "given the writer an official status," and "will gradually tend to make literature and art an integral part of the national life."

193   Godine, Amy. "Notes Toward a Reappraisal of Depression Literature." *Prospects* (Great Britain) 5 (1980): 197-239.

Discusses three categories of Depression-era writing—radical political novels, bohemian novels, and documentaries. Includes writers who worked for the WPA programs, for example, John Steinbeck, Tille Olsen, Nelson Algren, and Edward Dahlberg.

194   Goldstein, Harold M. "Regional Barriers in the Utilization of Federal Aid: The Southeast in the 1930's." *Quarterly Review of Economics and Business*, 7:2 (1967): 65-70.

Examines the effect of the WPA on the Southeast. Claims that cultural resistance to the WPA was greater in the Southeast than in other areas.

195   Goodman, Walter. *The Committee: The Extraordinary Career of the House Committee on Un-American Activities.* New York, NY: Farrar, Straus and Giroux, 1968. 564 pp.

Before the Dies Committee opened hearings in August, 1938, Parnell Thomas demanded "a sweeping investigation of the W.P.A.'s Federal Theatre and Writers' Project." He claimed that the project was "a hotbed for Communists" and "infested with radicals."

196   Goodson, Martia Graham. "An Introductory Essay and Subject Index to Selected Interviews from the Slave Narrative Collection." Ph.D. dissertation, Union Graduate School [Ohio], 1977.

197   Gottschalk, Louis, Clyde Kluckhohn and Robert Angell. *The Use of Personal Documents in History, Anthropology, and Sociology.* Foreword by Robert Redfield. New York, NY: Social Science Research Council, [1945]. 243 pp.

This book delineates the different types of personal documents (business records, government documents, letters) and explains their usefulness in historical analysis. It goes on to explain how an analysis comes about, how to secure information, how to tell the truth from falsehoods, etc. It does much the same sort of thing that Vansina does with oral tradition. Essay number two deals with personal histories in anthropology, and essay number three deals with sociology.

198   Govan, Sandra Y. "After the Renaissance: Gwendolyn Bennett and the WPA Years." *NAWA Review* [Baltimore, MD] 3:2 (December 1988): 27-31.

199   Graham, Joe. "Slave Narratives, Slave Culture, and the Slave Experience." In *The Emergence of Black English: Text and Commentary*, pp. 133-154, edited by Guy Bailey, Natalie Maynor, and Patricia Cukor-Avila. Amsterdam: John Benjamins, 1991.

Notes that the disc-recorded narratives collected by the Archive of Folk Song must be put into "the broader context" of the ex-slave narratives collected by the Federal Writers' Project. States that the disc recordings are "idiosyncratic in that each narrative reflects one individual's experiences...[that] are not representative of the experiences...of other slaves." Examines such aspects of slave life as slaves as chattel, attitudes toward masters, slave occupations, and folk narratives.

200   *The Great Depression: A Historical Bibliography*. Santa Barbara, CA: ABC-Clio Information Services, 1984.

201   Green, Archie. "The Archive's Shores." *Folklife Annual* (1985): 60-73.

Discusses the influence on folklore of three of Barrett Wendell's students—Robert Winslow Gordon, John Avery Lomax, and Horace Meyer Kallen. Notes that their work led to the founding of the American Folklife Center.

202   Gurko, Leo. *The Angry Decade*. New York, NY: Harper & Row, 1968. 306 pp. [Originally published in 1947.]

Includes brief comments about the FWP with a focus on the benefits for artists. Claims that "the artist applying for a WPA job had only to fill out a questionnaire and testify that he needed it...He remained...a free man; and though paid, his integrity as an artist was not part of the purchase price."

203   Gutheim, Frederick. "America in Guide Books." *Saturday Review of Literature*, 14 June 1941, p. 5

Presents a positive view of the American Guide Series of the Federal Writers' Project as the last state guide from Oklahoma was published. "I will certify that travel with and without the Guides is like dentistry before and after x-ray."

204   Gutman, Herbert G. *The Black Family in Slavery and Freedom, 1750-1925*. 1st ed. New York, NY: Pantheon Books, 1976. 664 pp.

205   Hamilton, Dona Cooper. "The National Urban League and New
       Deal Programs." *The Social Service Review* 58 (June 1984):
       227-243.
       Examines the preferences of the National Urban League about
       work relief programs, including more federal control and less
       local control, jobs rather than relief, the hiring of black
       administrators.

206   Hamilton, Virginia V. *Alabama Review* 36 (July 1983): 220-221.
       Review of *Up before Daylight: Life Histories from the Ala-
       bama Writers' Project, 1938-1939*, by James Seay Brown.
       [University, AL: University of Alabama Press, 1982. 261 pp.]

207   Hansen, Erik A. "The New Deal." In *Six American Novels: From
       New Deal to New Frontier. A Workbook*, edited by Jens Bogh
       and Steffen Skovmand, pp. 11-40. Aarhus: Akademisk
       Boghandel, 1972. 337 pp.

208   Harrison, Lowell H. "The Folklore of Some Kentucky Slaves."
       Kentucky Folklore Record 17:2 (1971): 25-30.

209   Harrison, Lowell H. "Memories of Slavery Days in Kentucky."
       Filson Club History Quarterly 47:3 (1973): 242-257.
       Quotes extensively from the ex-slave narratives to explain
       housing, food, punishment, and attitudes toward freedom.

210   Harrison, Lowell H. "Recollections of Some Tennessee Slaves."
       Tennessee Historical Quarterly 33:2 (1974): 175-190.
       Discusses the ex-slave interviews collected by the Federal
       Writers' Project in the 1930s.

211   Hart, Henry, ed. *The Writer in a Changing World*. New York,
       NY: Equinox Cooperative Press, 1937.

212   Hemenway, Robert. "Folklore Field Notes From Zora Neale
       Hurston." *Black Scholar* 7:7 (1976): 39-46.
       Includes Hurston's notes about a proposed but unfinished
       book on *Negroes in Florida*, a book she began editing while
       working with the Federal Writers' Project in Florida.

213   Hendrickson, Gordon O. "The WPA Writers' Project in Wyo-
       ming: History and Collections." *Annals of Wyoming* 49:2
       (Fall 1977): 175-192.
       Discusses the problems and accomplishments of the Federal
       Writer's Project in producing the state guides and other
       publications under the direction first of Mart Christensen and
       Agnes Wright Spring. Explains the detailed inventory of the
       WPA material in the Wyoming State Archives, including

manuscripts, photographs, and administrative papers of the Historical Records Survey and the Federal Writers' Project.

214 Hendrickson, Kenneth E., Jr. "The WPA Arts Projects in Texas." *East Texas Historical Journal* 26:2 (1988): 3-13.

Discusses the activities of the Federal Writers' Project, Federal Theatre Project, the Federal Music Project, and the Federal Art Project.

215 Hersey, John, ed. *Ralph Ellison: A Collection of Critical Essays.* Twentieth Century Views Series. A Spectrum Book. Englewood Cliffs, NJ: Prentice-Hall, 1974. 180 pp.

216 Hessler, Marilyn S. "Marcus Christian: The Man and His Collection." *Louisiana History* 28:1 (1987): 37-55.

Notes that Christian worked as a local project director in the Federal Writers' Project. Discusses his large collection of poetry and black history, material which is deposited at the University of New Orleans.

217 Hicken, Victor. *Journal of the Illinois State Historical Society* 68 (September 1975): 376.

Review of *Roosevelt's Image Brokers: Poets, Playwrights and the Use of the Lincoln Symbol,* by Alfred Haworth Jones. [Port Washington, NY: Kennikat Press, 1974.]

218 Hirsch, Jerrold. "Cultural Pluralism and Applied Folklore: The New Deal Precedent." In *The Conservation of Culture,* edited by Burt Feintuch, pp. 46-67. Publications of the American Folklore Society, New Series, No. 5. Lexington, KY: University Press of Kentucky, 1988.

States that central questions for the guidebook essays included "the artist's relationship to his culture" and "the possibility of creating an indigenous American art," as part of the effort to "reconcile pluralist ideas with modernism as well as romanticism." Notes that "the Depression led Botkin to explore increasingly the social relevance of folklore and literature."

219 Hirsch, Jerrold. "Cultural Pluralism and the Conservation of Southern Culture: The New Deal Precedent." In *Cultural Heritage Conservation in the American South,* edited by Benita J. Howell, pp. 20-33. Southern Anthropological Society Proceedings, Series No. 23. Athens, GA: University of Georgia Press, 1990. 143 pp.

220   Hirsch, Jerrold M. "Culture on Relief: The Federal Writers' Project in North Carolina, 1935-1942." M.A. thesis, University of North Carolina at Chapel Hill, 1973.

221   Hirsch, Jerrold M. "Folklore in the Making: B. A. Botkin." *Journal of American Folklore* 100:3 (January-March 1987): 36.

222   Hirsch, Jerrold. "Modernity, Nostalgia, and Southern Folklore Studies: The Case of John Lomax." *Journal of American Folklore* 105 (Spring 1992): 183-207.

       States that in order to understand John Lomax, who served as folklore editor of the Federal Writers' Project in 1936-1937, "it is necessary to examine the intersection between his outlook as a racially conservative white Southerner and his outlook as a folklorist." Contrasts the views and work of John Lomax with those of Benjamin Botkin and Alan Lomax.

223   Hirsch, Jerrold M. "Portrait of America: The Federal Writers' Project in an Intellectual and Cultural Context." Ph.D. dissertation, University of North Carolina at Chapel Hill, 1984.

       States that the Federal Writers' Project officials "through the study of the experience and cultural expressions of ordinary Americans could provide the basis for a revitalized national culture." This important study includes such topics as the American Guide books, the Dies Committee and the FWP, the ideas and contributions of Benjamin Botkin, oral history research, and Ralph Ellison and the FWP.

224   Hirsch, Jerrold. "Reading and Counting." *Reviews in American History* 8 (1980): 312-317.

       Review essay of *Slavery Remembered: A Record of Twentieth-Century Slave Narratives*, by Paul D. Escott. [Chapel Hill: University of North Carolina Press, 1979.]

225   Hirsch, Jerrold and Tom E. Terrill. "Conceptualization and Implementation: Some Thoughts on Reading the Federal Writers' Project Southern Life Histories." *Southern Studies* 18:3 (1979): 351-362.

       Explains some of the problems that historians must be aware of in working with the life histories of southerners collected by the Federal Writers' Project in the 1930s. Describes the collection of ex-slave narratives, folklore, and folksong.

226   Hoagland, Edward. "The WPA Guide to New York City." *New York Times Book Review*, 21 November 1982, Section 7, p. 3, 28-29.

227   Hobson, Archie, ed. *Remembering America: A Sampler of the WPA American Guide Series.* Introduction by Bill Stott. New York, NY: Columbia University Press, 1985. 391 pp. Reprinted New York, NY: Macmillan, 1987. 411 pp.

228   Hopkins, Harry L. *Spending to Save: The Complete Story of Relief.* New York, NY: W. W. Norton, 1936. 197 pp. Reprinted Americana Library, No. 23. Introduction by Roger Daniels. Seattle, WA: University of Washington Press, 1972. 197 pp.

Discusses the principles and policies of relief and work programs. Important as source of general information about context and ideas by the administrator of the WPA program rather than as a study of the Federal Writers' program.

229   Horlings, Albert. "Guidebooks to America." *New Republic,* 13 April 1942, p. 501.

Describes the state Guides as individual items as "competent, readable" rather than "extraordinary." However, "when one looks at the Guides in the large, most criticism becomes picayunish." John D. Newsom, then director of the FWP, noted that a former FWP member wrote a letter stating that the publication of his first novel "would have been impossible without the FWP."

230   Houston, Maude. "The Education of John A. Lomax." *Southwestern Historical Quarterly* 60:2 (1956-1957): 201-218.

Presents information about the formal education of this well-known collector of folklore and folk music. Covers the period from the early 1880s to 1897, the year that John Lomax was graduated from the University of Texas.

231   Howard, Donald S. *The WPA and Federal Relief Policy.* New York, NY: Russell Sage Foundation, 1943. Reprinted New York, NY: Da Capo, 1973. 888 pp.

Explains that in some areas boards were set up to evaluate works "submitted by candidates for employment on art, writers', or comparable projects." Notes that in 1936 Richard Wright submitted his writings to such a board and was transferred from manual labor projects to a writers' project. "This was just two years before his 'Uncle Tom's Children' won a first prize conducted by a national magazine for employes [sic] of WPA writers' project, and some four years before his *Native Son,* a best seller, appeared."

232   Howell, Elmo. "William Faulkner and the New Deal." *Midwest Quarterly: A Journal of Contemporary Thought* [Pittsburg, KS] 5 (1964): 323-332.

233   Hudson, John C. "The Study of Western Frontier Populations." In *The American West: New Perspectives, New Dimensions*, pp. 35-60. Introduction by Jerome O. Steffen. Norman, OK: University of Oklahoma Press, 1979. 238 pp.

234   Huffman, Laurie. "The WPA Project As Humanistic Experience." *Pacific History*, 27:4 (1983): 4-9.

       Stresses the value of the work of the Federal Writers' Project, Federal Theater Project, Federal Music Project, and the Historical Records Survey. Notes that the community provided part of the cost of the project; the WPA provided the work needed by the community.

235   Humphreys, Hubert. "Oral History Research in Louisiana: An Overview." *Louisiana History* 20:4 (Fall 1979): 353-371.

       Notes in this Presidential address to the Louisiana Historical Association that many narratives collected by the WPA in the 1930s have been used in historical research. Claims that tape-recorded interviews were first used extensively for historical research in the 1950s.

236   Hunt, Byron. *From Alphabetical Soup to WPA Nuts*, Indianapolis, IN: M. Miller, 1939. 220 pp.

237   Hurmence, Belinda, ed. *Before Freedom When I Just Can Remember*. New York, NY: Blair, 1988. 135 pp.

       Includes 27 slave narratives collected by the Federal Writers' Project in South Carolina, edited by the author of the book. Presents the ex-slaves' views of masters, homes, and celebrations during the time of slavery.

238   Ingram, Elwanda D. "Willard Motley's *Knock on Any Door*: An Outgrowth of the WPA." *NAWA Review* [Baltimore, MD.] 3:2 (December 1988): 39-42.

239   *Inventory of W.P.A. Papers in the Louisiana Collection of the Louisiana State Library*. Baton Rouge, LA: The Library, 1970. Photocopy.

240   Jackson, Bruce. "Benjamin A. Botkin (1901-1975)." *Journal of American Folklore* 89 (1976): 1-6.

241   Jackson, Bruce, ed. *Folklore and Society: Essays in Honor of Ben Botkin*. Hatboro, PA: Folklore Associates, 1966.

Includes a chronological listing of Botkin's publications, many of them written during the period of the New Deal and the WPA.

242   Jackson, David. "Black Artists and the WPA." *Encore*, 19 November 1979, p. 22.

243   Jacobs, Donald M. *Index to the American Slave*. Westport, CT: Greenwood Press, 1981.

Includes such information as the name, age, sex, job or work done, place of interview, and other information that will be useful to researchers in many fields.

244   Jacobs, Donald M. "Twentieth-Century Slave Narratives as Source Materials: Slave Labor as Agricultural Labor." *Agricultural History*, 57:2 (April 1983): 223-227.

The ex-slave studies project of the Federal Writers' Project collected interviews in 26 states in the late 1930s. Explains the purpose and organization of his index to the 3,500 interviews collected.

245   Jellison, Charles A. *Tomatoes Were Cheaper: Tales from the Thirties*. Syracuse, NY: Syracuse University Press, 1977. 240 pp.

Relates tales about and explains the cultural context of the WPA, including the Federal Writers' Project. Particularly interesting is the story of how Harry Hopkins persuaded President Roosevelt to set up arts programs under the WPA after hearing the story about a frail man who died soon after taking a job to dig a drainage ditch in Chicago.

246   Johns, Orrick. *Time of Our Lives: The Story of My Father and Myself*. New York, NY: Stackpole, 1937.

Deals with the writer's experience in working with the Federal Writers' Project.

247   Johnson, Gerri. "Maryland Roots: An Examination of the Free State's WPA Ex-Slave Narratives." *Free State Folklore* 4:1 (1977): 18-34.

248   Johnson, Jerah. "Marcus B. Christian and the WPA History of Black People in Louisiana." *Louisiana History* 20 (1979): 113-115.

Notes that Marcus B. Christian, director of the Federal Writers' Project at Dillard University, worked on a history of blacks in Louisiana. Notes that the materials are deposited at the University of New Orleans.

249   Jones, Alfred Haworth. *Roosevelt's Image Brokers: Poets, Play-wrights and the Use of the Lincoln Symbol.* National University Publications Series in American Studies. Port Washington, NY: Kennikat Press, 1974. 134 pp.

250   Jones, Alfred Haworth. "The Search for a Usable American Past in the New Deal Era." *American Quarterly* 23:35 (December 1971): 710-724.

"After 1933, the government-sponsored cultural projects furthered an adventure in national rediscovery which represented one of the most far-reaching developments of the Depression decade."

251   Jones, J. Ralph. "Portraits of Georgia Slaves." *Georgia Review* 21 (1967): 126-132.

252   *Journal of Library History* 20 (Fall 1985): 455.

Review of *Pickaxe and Pencil: References for the Study of the WPA,* by Marguerite D. Bloxom. [Washington, DC: Library of Congress, 1982. 87 pp.]

253   *Journal of the West* 26 (July 1987): 104.

Review of *The WPA Guide to Texas,* edited by Robert A. Calvert and Anne Hodges Morgan. Reprint ed. [originally published in 1940].

254   Joyner, Charles. *Down by the Riverside: A South Carolina Slave Community.* Urbana and Chicago, IL: University of Illinois Press, 1984. 345 pp.

Uses the slave narrative interviews collected by the Federal Writers' Project as an important source in studying African and European-American influences on the development of community among slaves who worked on rice plantations along the South Carolina coast. An important and very readable study of how the slaves adapted elements of these influences in creating the Gullah language, religion, and work patterns. Shows that the ex-slave narratives collected by the Federal Writers' Project are a valuable resource for the cultural historian.

255   Joyner, Charles W. "Soul Food and the Sambo Stereotype: Foodlore From the Slave Narrative Collection." *Keystone Folklore Quarterly* 16 (1971): 171-178.

256   Kalmar, Karen L. "Southern Black Elites and the New Deal: A Case Study of Savannah, Georgia." *Georgia Historical Quarterly* 65:4 (Winter 1981): 341-355.

Note that the author's name is listed as Kolmar on the contents page, as Kalmar in the article. Discusses discrimination against lower-class blacks in Savannah. Complaints to the national WPA office were referred back to the state WPA office, a procedure that typically did not result in solving the problem.

257 Kaplan, Sam Hill. "The WPA Guide to New York City." Review. *Los Angeles Times,* 7 November 1982, Section B, p. 10.

258 Keller, Morton, ed. *The New Deal: What Was It?* American Problem Studies. New York, NY: Holt, Rinehart and Winston, 1963. 122 pp.

259 Kellock, Katherine. "The WPA Writers: Portraitists of the United States." *American Scholar* 9 (October 1940): 473-482.

The FWP guides "reveal an America that neither the historians nor the imaginative writers of the past had discovered," and the guides "present a vast amount of new regional material that other writers are already incorporating in articles, stories and books."

260 Kendrick, Dolores. *The Women of Plums: Poems in the Voices of Slave Women.* New York, NY: Morrow, 1989. 96 pp.

Creates stories for 34 black slave women whose stories are told in poetic monologues based on the ex-slave recordings in the Library of Congress.

261 Kernan, Michael. "Memories of Slave Days." *Washington Post,* 7 November 1969.

262 Kifer, Allen Francis. "The Negro Under the New Deal." Ph.D. dissertation, University of Wisconsin, 1961.

263 "Killing the Writers' Project." *New Republic,* 23 August 1969, p. 62.

264 Kirsch, Jonathan. "WPA Guide to California." Review. *Los Angeles Times,* 22 April 1984, *The Book Review,* p. 4.

265 Kliger, Hannah, ed. *Jewish Hometown Associations & Family Circles in New York: The WPA Yiddish Writers' Group Study.* The Modern Jewish Experience Series. Bloomington, IN: Indiana University Press, 1992. 208 pp.

266 Knight, Thomas. *Journal of the West* 13 (July 1974): 120.

Review of *San Francisco: A Guide to the Bay and Its Cities.* Revised edition. [New York, NY: Hastings House, 1973. 470 pp.]

267   Koenig, Rhoda. "WPA Guides." *New York*, 4-11 July 1983,
       p. 115.

268   Kolchin, Peter. *First Freedom: The Responses of Alabama's
       Blacks to Emancipation and Reconstruction.* Contributions in
       American History, No. 20. Westport, CT: Greenwood Press,
       1972. 215 pp.

269   Kostiainen, Auvo. "The Portrait of Finnish Americans: Materials
       on the Minnesota Finns Collected by the WPA Writers'
       Project." [Amerikansuomalaisten Kuva: Tyottomyystyona a
       Tallennettua Minnesotan Suomalaisten Historiaa.] *Turun
       Hist. Arkisto* (Finland) 31 (1976): 414-431.
       Analyzes the 143 interviews collected from first and second
       generation Finns in Minnesota. Notes that the inverviews
       contain information about why the Finns emigrated, when
       they arrived in America, their occupations, their education,
       and their social activities.

270   Kurzman, Paul A. *Harry Hopkins and the New Deal.* Foreword
       by Louis W. Koenig. Fair Lawn, NJ: R. E. Burdick, 1974.
       219 pp.

271   Landers, Clifford E. and Arthur E. Nudelman. "Professors, Poli-
       tics and the Government." *Midwest Quarterly* 14:1 (October
       1972): 41-51.
       Suggests the federal government set up a "permanent agency
       somewhat on the model of the Works Progress Administra-
       tion to investigate the chronic problems that confront Amer-
       ica." Notes the availability of a record number of individuals
       trained in graduate schools "despite the ready evidence of a
       job shortage."

272   Lane, Ann J. *The Debate Over Slavery.* Urbana, IL: University
       of Illinois Press, 1971.
       Presents a collection of essays that examine and evaluate
       many of the ideas and comments by Stanley Elkins—com-
       parisons Elkins made between U.S. slavery, slavery in Cuba
       and Central America, and the German concentration camps;
       Elkins' belief in a "sambo-mentality" among black slaves.

273   Lantz, Herman R. "Family and Kin as Revealed in the Narratives
       of Ex-Slaves." *Social Science Quarterly* 60:4 (March 1980):
       667-675.
       Analyzes the ex-slave interviews in order to determine the
       effect of slavery on the African American family in America.

Supports the view that before the Civil War the family was more stable than researchers had earlier thought was the case.

274   Larson, Cedric. "Uncle Sam, Printer, Publisher and Literary Sponsor." *Colophon* 1 (1939): 83-90.

275   Lawrence, Ken. "Oral History of Slavery." *Southern Exposure* 1:4 (1974): 84-86.

Claims that black historians at Southern University and Fisk University developed oral history during the 1920s in order to interview ex-slaves. The Federal Writers' Project continued the collection of interviews in the 1930s.

276   Lawson, Alan. "The Cultural Legacy of the New Deal." In *Fifty Years Later: The New Deal Evaluated,* edited by Harvard Sitkoff, pp. 155-186. Philadelphia, PA: Temple University Press, 1985.

Claims that the New Deal arts projects had "tapped some great wellspring" with the Federal Writers' Project offering "desperately poor novices...[such as] Edward Dahlberg, Ralph Ellison, Richard Wright, Saul Bellow, and Eudora Welty, the chance to prepare for professional careers."

277   Lear, Linda J. *Journal of the West* 25 (October 1986): 75.

Review of *The WPA Guide to America: The Best of 1930s America as Seen by the Federal Writers' Project,* by Bernard A. Weisberger. [New York, NY: Pantheon Books, 1985. 449 pp.]

278   Leuchtenburg, William E[dward]. *Franklin D. Roosevelt and the New Deal, 1932-1940.* 1st ed. The New American Nation series. New York, NY: Harper & Row, 1963. 393 pp.

279   Leuchtenburg, William E[dward], ed. *The New Deal: A Documentary History.* Columbia, SC: University of South Carolina Press, 1968. 263 pp.

280   Levine, Lawrence W. "Slave Songs and Slave Conciousness: An Exploration in Neglected Sources." *Anonymous Americans: Explorations in Nineteenth Century History.* Edited by Tamara Hareven. Englewood Cliffs, NJ: Prentice-Hall, 1971.

281   Liasson, Mara. "The Federal Writers' Project and the Folklore of Cultural Pluralism." B.A. thesis, Brown University, 1977.

282   Linzee, Jill Inman. *A Reference Guide to Florida Folklore from the Federal WPA Deposited in the Florida Folklife Archives.* [Tallahassee, FL]: Florida Department of State, Division of Historical Resources, Bureau of Florida Folklife Programs, 1990.

283   Lipscomb, Lena. "Jacksboro Ghost Tales from the WPA Archives." Charles [K.] Wolfe, ed. and introduction. *East Tennessee Folklore Society Bulletin* 50:2 (1984): 68-74.

284   *Literary Writings in America: A Bibliography*. 8 vols. Millwood, NY: KTO Press, 1977.

       Publishes the card file of American literature compiled by workers for the Historical Records Survey working at the University of Pennsylvania. Represents the "result of photo-offsetting the entire card catalog...as it existed when the project was terminated in 1942."

285   Littell, Robert. "Putting America on Paper." *Today*, 30 November 1935, pp. 6-9.

286   Litwack, Leon. *Been in the Storm So Long: The Aftermath of Slavery*. New York, NY: Knopf, 1979. 651 pp.

       Discusses the final phase of slavery, based on slaves' testimony. Denies Stanley Elkins' Sambo thesis and disagrees with Eugene Genovese's claim that southerners did not feel any guilt about slavery.

287   Lomax, Alan. "Vanishing American Lingoes: The Media Threat to Our Native Gift of Gab." *Family Heritage* 1:2 (1978): 34-38.

       Tells about his experiences as a collector of stories, oral histories, and songs. Claims that radio and television have imposed a standardization of the language that discourages innovation in speech.

288   Lomax, John A. "Field Experience with Recording Machines." *Southern Folklore Quarterly* 1 (1937): 57-60.

289   Loomis, John P. "Reds and Rackets in Work Relief." *Saturday Evening Post*, 5 June 1937, pp. 25, 97-98, 100-104.

290   Louchheim, Katie, ed. *The Making of the New Deal: The Insiders Speak*. Historical notes by Jonathan Dembo. Cambridge, MA: Harvard University Press, 1983. 368 pp.

291   Lovell, John. *Black Song: The Forge and the Flame*. New York: Macmillan, 1972.

292   Lovell, Linda Jeanne. "African-American Narratives from Arkansas: A Study from the 1936-1938 Federal Writers' Project." Ph.D. dissertation, University of Arkansas, 1991.

       Focuses on the 696 interviews collected by the Federal Writers' Project in Arkansas, comprising almost one-third of the original collection. Stresses the historical importance of the narratives and "the literary merit of the collection." Asserts that the narratives are important to creative writers.

293 Lowitt, Richard. *The New Deal and the West*. The West in the Twentieth Century series. Bloomington, IN: Indiana University Press, 1984. 283 pp.

294 MacLeish, Archibald. "He Cherished American Culture." *New Republic*, 15 April 1946, p. 540-541.

Praises President Roosevelt's decision to set up relief agencies in the arts. They served as a "declaration...that those who follow learning and the arts are as important to the Republic as those who follow other callings...." Notes that the state Guides are an example of work with lasting value.

295 MacLeish, Archibald. *Land of the Free*. New York, NY: Harcourt, Brace and Company, 1938.

Reprinted, with introduction by A. D. Coleman. New York, NY: Da Capo Press, 1977.

Poem written in July and August of 1937 to illustrate a book of photographs, "most of them taken for the Resettlement Administration, which later became the Farm Security Administration." Presents a visual and verbal picture of the 1930s and the Great Depression.

296 MacLeod, Bruce A. "Quills, Fifes, and Flutes Before the Civil War." *Southern Folklore Quarterly* 42: 2-3 (1978): 201-208.

Uses the ex-slave narratives collected by the Federal Writers' Project as as source of information.

297 Macleod, Norman. *You Get What You Ask For*. New York, NY: Harrison-Hilton, 1939.

Deals with the writers' experiences with the Federal Writers' Project.

298 Macmahon, Arthur W[hittier], John D. Millett and Gladys Ogden. *The Administration of Federal Work Relief*. Studies in Administration, Vol. 12. Chicago, IL: Public Administration Service, for the Committee on Public Administration of the Social Science Research Council, 1941. 407 pp.

Reprinted Da Capo Press Reprint Edition. *Franklin D. Roosevelt and the Era of the New Deal*. Frank Freidel, General Editor. New York, NY: Da Capo Press, 1971. 407 pp.

299 Macnaughtan, Don, compiler. *Oregon Oddities: Intriguing Items From the Files of the WPA Writers' Project*. Eugene, OR: Eugene Public Library, 1986.

300   "Make-work." *Washington Post,* 26 November 1984, Section A,
         p. 14.
         An editorial that recognizes WPA projects of lasting worth.

301   Mangione, Jerre [Gerlando]. *The Dream and the Deal: The
         Federal Writers' Project, 1935-1943.* 1st ed. Boston, MA:
         Little, Brown and Company, 1972. 416 pp.
         New York, NY: Avon, 1974. Philadelphia, PA: University of
             Pennsylvania Press, 1983. 432 pp.
         Philadelphia, PA: University of Pennsylvania Press, 1983.
             416 pp. paper.

302   Mangione, Jerre. "Federal Writers' Project." *New York Times,* 18
         May 1969, Section 7, pp. 2, 32.

303   Marcello, Ronald E. "The Politics of Relief: The North Carolina
         WPA and the Tar Heel Elections of 1936." *North Carolina
         Historical Review* 68:1 (January 1991).

304   March, Michael S. "Poverty: How Much Will the War Cost?"
         Social Service Review 39:2 (1965): 141-156.
         Discusses the "War on Poverty" in relation to the WPA
         programs. Claims that "investment in human resources" is
         one approach available to government control.

305   Mathews, Jane De Hart. "Arts and the People: The New Deal
         Quest for a Cultural Democracy." *Journal of American His-
         tory* 62:2 (1975): 316-339.
         New Deal projects in music, theatre, art, and writing tried to
         make cultural events accessible to the public and encouraged
         the development of a national art. Bureaucracy and political
         opposition made it difficult for the projects to accomplish
         their goals.

306   Maw, Herbert B. "In Memoriam: Marguerite L. Sinclair Reusser
         1895-1976." *Utah Historical Quarterly* 44:4 (Fall 1976):
         397-398.
         Recognizes the contribution of Marguerite L. S. Reusser
         (1898-1976) to the collecting or transcribing of historical
         materials by the WPA in Utah.

307   Maxwell, Fay. *Lake County, Ohio History Plus Lake County
         WPA History Index.* Columbus, Ohio: Ohio Genealogy Cen-
         ter, 1984. 4 pp.

308   Maynor, Natalie. "The WPA Slave Narratives Revisited." *Ameri-
         can Speech* 66 (Spring 1991): 82-86.

Review of *American Earlier Black English* by Edgar W. Schneider. [University, AL: University of Alabama Press, 1989.]

309 Maynor, Natalie. "Written Records of Spoken Language: How Reliable Are They?" In *Methods in Dialectology*, edited by Allan Thomas, pp. 109-119. London: Multicultural Matters, 1988.

Compares versions of three of the ex-slave narratives in the Rawick 1972 and Rawick 1979 collections. [See *The American Slave: A Composite Autobiography*.] Suggests that the narratives might be viewed as a literary source.

310 McCauley, Michael J. *Jim Thompson: Sleep with the Devil*. New York, NY: Mysterious Press, 1991.

Biography of Jim Thompson (1906-1977), a crime novelist from Oklahoma, who was a writer with the WPA.

311 McCoy, Garnett. *American Historical Review* 80:2 (April 75): 527-528.

Review of *Art for the Millions: Essays from the 1930's by Artists and Administrators of the WPA Federal Art Project*, by Francis V. O'Connor [Greenwich, CT: New York Graphic Society, 1973. 317 pp.] and *The New Deal for Artists*, by Richard D. McKinzie [Princeton: Princeton University Press, 1973. 203 pp.].

312 McDonald, Donald. *Center Magazine* 17:1 (March-April 1984): 43-44.

Reviews WPA Guides for New York City, Massachusetts, Washington, DC, Illinois, and New Orleans.

313 McDonald, Forrest, and Grady McWhiney. "The Antebellum Southern Herdsman: A Reinterpretation." *Journal of Southern History* 41 (1975): 147-66.

314 McDonald, William Francis. *Federal Relief Administration and the Arts: The Origins and Administrative History of the Arts Projects of the Works Progress Administration*. Columbus, OH: Ohio State University Press, 1969. 883 pp.

315 McElvaine, Robert S. *Down and Out in the Great Depression: Letters from the Forgotten Man*. Chapel Hill, NC: University of North Carolina Press, 1983. 251 pp.

316 McElvaine, Robert S. *The Great Depression: America, 1929-1941*. New York, NY: Times Book, 1984. 402 pp.

317   McFarland, Keith D. *Journal of the West* 26 (January 1987): 91-92.

        Review of *Remembering America: A Sampler of the WPA American Guide Series*, edited by Archie Hobson. [New York, NY: Columbia University Press, 1985. 391 pp.]

318   McLaughlin, Doris B. "Putting Michigan Back To Work." *Michigan History*, 66:1 (1982): 30-37.

319   McKenna, James F. "Narrative Reports from the WPA." *Spinner: People and Culture in Southeastern Massachusetts* 4 (1988): 26-33.

        Presents Federal Writers' Project report about projects of the Civil Works Administration, the Works Progress Administration, and the Federal Emergency Relief Administration in New Bedford, Massachusetts.

320   McKinzie, Kathleen O'Connor. "Writers on Relief: 1935-1942." Ph.D. dissertation, Indiana University, 1970.

321   McKinzie, Richard. *Annals of Iowa* 49 (Spring 1989): 725-726.

        Review of *The WPA Guide to 1930s Iowa*, originally published as *Iowa: A Guide to the Hawkeye State*, 1938. Federal Writers' Project. [Ames, IA: Iowa State University Press, 1986. 583 pp.]

322   McKinzie, Richard. *Annals of Iowa* 49 (Spring 1989): 725-726.

        Review of *Remembering America: A Sampler of the WPA American Guide Series*, edited by Archie Hobson. [New York, NY: Columbia University Press, 1985. 391 pp.]

323   McKinzie, Richard D. *The New Deal for Artists*. Princeton, NJ: Princeton University Press, 1973. 203 pp.

324   McKinzie, Richard D. "The New Deal for Artists: Federal Subsidies, 1933-1943." Dissertation, Indiana University, 1969.

325   McNutt, James Charles. "Beyond Regionalism: Texas Folklorists and the Emergence of a Post-Regional Consciousness." Ph.D. dissertation, University of Texas at Austin, 1982. 394 pp.

        Analyzes the work and influence of John A. Lomax, J. Frank Dobie, and Moody Boatright.

326   McNutt, James. "John Henry Faulk: An Interview." *Folklife Annual* (1987): 106-109.

Presents John Henry Faulk's views about folklore and comments about his work with folklorists John Lomax and Alan Lomax.

327   McPherson, Milton. *Alabama Review* 35 (April 1982): 147-149.
       Review of *Toting the Lead Row: Ruby Pickens Tartt, Alabama Folklorist*, by Virginia Pounds Brown and Laurella Owens. [University, AL: University of Alabama Press, 1981. 180 pp.]

328   McSweeney, Kerry. *Invisible Man*. Twayne's Masterwork Studies, 17. New York, NY: Twayne Publishers, 1988. 139 pp.

329   Mehren, Peter. "The San Diego City Schools Curriculum Project of the WPA." *Journal of San Diego History* 18:2 (1972): 8-14.
       Notes that WPA writers provided text and drawings about San Diego. Relates the story about how in 1935 Dr. Jay D. Conmer saw a famous writer working as manual laborer and then suggested to the Superintendent of Schools that writers could be more effectively employed by providing texts that could be used in the schools.

330   Mellon, James, ed. *Bullwhip Days: The Slaves Remember*. New York, NY: Grove and Weidenfeld, 1989. 448 pp. New York, NY: Grove-Atlantic, 1989. New York: Avon, 1990. 480 pp. paper.
       A collection of 29 ex-slave narratives, selected from the Library of Congress volume to document the conditions of slavery.

331   Meltzer, Milton. *Violins and Shovels: The WPA Arts Projects*. New York, NY: Delacorte Press, 1976.

332   Mercer, P. M. "Tapping the Slave Narrative Collection for the Responses of Black South Carolinians to Emancipation and Reconstruction." *Australian Journal of Politics and History* 25:3 (1979): 358-374.

333   Millay, Edna St. Vincent. "Famous Poet Condemns Cuts." In *WPA Defender*, p. 4. New York, 1937.

334   "Mirror to America." *Time*, 3 January 1938, pp. 55-56.
       Describes the Federal Writers' Project as "the biggest literary job ever undertaken," "a gigantic job of holding the mirror up to the face of the U. S.," with one thing already being taught—"how little [readers] know about their vast and uncharted country." Refers to the work of Conrad Aiken, Vardis Fisher, Lyle Saxon, Ross Santee, J. Frank Davis, Reed Harris, Edward Barrows, Orrick Johns, and Jack Conroy.

335   Mitchell, Broadus. *Depression Decade: From New Era through New Deal, 1929-1941*. The Economic History of the United States, Vol. 9. New York, NY: Rinehart, 1947. 462 pp.

336   Mizruchi, Ephraim H. *Regulating Society: Marginality and Social Control in Historical Perspective*. New York, NY: The Free Press, 1983. 207 pp.

       Examines the ways in which societies have contained or regulated dissident groups by setting up special organizations. Discusses in Chapter 6 the factors which influenced the government to set up WPA writers' and artists' projects.

337   Moltke-Hansen, David. *North Carolina Historical Review* 67 (April 1990): 253.

       Review of *South Carolina: The WPA Guide to the Palmetto State*. [Columbia, SC: University of South Carolina Press, 1988. 531 pp. Reprint of the 1941 publication by the Federal Writers' Project.]

338   Montell, William Lynwood. *The Saga of Coe Ridge: A Study in Oral History*. Knoxville, TN: The University of Tennessee Press, 1970. 231 pp.

       Discusses Coe Ridge, Kentucky located near the Tennessee border, a place where for nearly 100 years after emancipation, a group of freed slaves and occasional whites lived with little outside contact. Based in part on former slaves' accounts.

339   Montgomery, Michael B. and Guy Bailey. *Language Variety in the South: Perspectives in Black and White*. Foreword by James B. McMillan. University, AL: University of Alabama Press, 1986. 427 pp.

       Includes 23 papers, a few of which include reference to or analysis of the ex-slave narratives collected by the Federal Writers' Project. Focuses on the complex relationship between black varieties and white varieties of English spoken in the American South.

340   Montgomery, Michael. "The Linguistic Value of the Ex-Slave Recordings." In *The Emergence of Black English: Text and Commentary*, pp. 173-190, edited by Guy Bailey, Natalie Maynor and Patricia Cukor-Avila. Amsterdam: John Benjamins, 1991.

       Questions the reliability of the ex-slave narratives collected by the Federal Writers' Project as a source of information about language structure and use. Based on an analysis of two linguistic features, left dislocation and relative pronouns.

Montgomery concludes that the value of the ex-slave narratives "may well be limited to that of literary dialect."

341   Morreale, Ben. "Jerre Mangione: The Sicilian Sources." *Italian Americana* 7:1 (1981): 4-18.

Discusses Mangione's writing experiences with the Federal Writers' Project as part of a brief biography.

342   Morrison, Perry. "Everyman's Archive." *The Call* 18:2 (Spring 1957): 4-9.

343   Mufwene, Salikoko. *Journal of Pidgin and Creole Languages* 2 (1987): 93-110.

Review of *Language Variety in the South: Perspectives in Black and White,* edited by Michael Montgomery and Guy Bailey. [University, AL: University of Alabama Press, 1986. 427 pp.]

344   Mumford, Lewis. "A Letter to the President." *New Republic,* 30 December 1936, pp. 263-265.

345   Mumford, Lewis. "Writers' Project." *New Republic,* 20 October 1937, pp. 306-307.

"These guidebooks are the finest contribution to American patriotism that has been made in our generation....Future historians will turn to these guidebooks as one who would know the classic world must still turn to Pausanias' ancient guidebook to Greece."

346   Muraire, Andre. "The New Deal Mentality." In *A New Deal Reader,* pp. 21-35. Aix-en-Provence, France: Publications of the Université de Provence, 1983. 138 pp.

347   Myers, Robert Manson, ed. *The Children of Pride: A True Story of Georgia and the Civil War.* New Haven, CT: Yale University Press, 1972. 1845 pp.

348   Nadel, Alan. *Invisible Criticism: Ralph Ellison and the American Canon.* Iowa City, IA: University of Iowa Press, 1988. 181 pp.

349   Naison, Mark. "Communism and Harlem Intellectuals in the Popular Front: Anti-Fascism and the Politics of Black Culture." *Journal of Ethnic Studies* 9:1 (Spring 1981): 1-25.

Notes that the Communist Party gained prestige through its efforts to acquire support for black arts, focusing the efforts on the WPA project for artists and writing.

350   Nash, Horace D. "Blacks in Arkansas During Reconstruction:
       The Ex-Slave Narratives." *Arkansas Historical Quarterly* 48
       (1989): 243-259.
       Discusses experiences of Arkansas blacks during Reconstruc-
       tion, as well as harrassment by the Ku Klux Klan, their views
       of education, and their political participation.

351   "New in Paperback." *Washington Post,* 10 November 1985,
       Section 10, p. 12.
       Review of *The WPA Guide to America: The Best of 1930s
       America As Seen by the Federal Writers' Project,* edited by
       Bernard A. Weisberger [New York, NY: Pantheon, 1985].

352   Nicholas, H. G. "The Writer and the State." *Contemporary Re-
       view* 155 (January 1939): 89-94.
       "As Roosevelt's public works were to 'prime the pump' to
       prosperity, so the Federal Writers' Project would prime the
       pump to national self-awareness, both of the past and of the
       present."

353   "The 1930's." *Carleton Miscellany* [special issue] 6 (Winter
       1965).

354   Noah, Timothy. "Bring Back the WPA." *Washington Monthly,*
       19 September 1982, p. 38.

355   O'Gara, Geoffrey. *A Long Road Home: Journeys Through Amer-
       ica's Present in Search of America's Past.* New York, NY:
       Norton, 1989.
       Compares the America described in the state guides with his
       own impressions during his travel.

356   O'Gara, Geoffrey. *A Long Road Home: Travels Through Amer-
       ica Today with the Great 1930s WPA Guides.* Boston, MA:
       Houghton Mifflin, 1990. 352 pp. paper.

357   Ohl, John Kennedy. *Hugh S. Johnson and the New Deal.* Dekalb,
       IL: Northern Illinois University Press, 1985. 374 pp.

358   Olson, James S., ed. *Historical Dictionary of the New Deal: From
       Inauguration to Preparation for War.* Westport, CT: Green-
       wood Press, 1985. 611 pp.

359   O'Meally, Robert G. *New Essays on Invisible Man.* Cambridge:
       Cambridge University Press, 1988. 190 pp.

360   O'Neal, Hank. *A Vision Shared: A Classic Portrait of America
       and Its People, 1935-1943.* New York, NY: St. Martin's
       Press, 1976.

361   O'Neill, Robert K. "The Federal Writers' Project Files For Indiana." *Indiana Magazine of History* 76:2 (1980): 85-96.

362   Orvell, Miles. "Letting the Facts Speak For Themselves: Thirties America." *American Scholar* 43:4 (Autumn 1974): 671-678.
       Reviews *Portrait of a Decade: Roy Stryker and the Development of Documentary Photography in the Thirties,* by F. Jack Hurley, *Documentary Expression and Thirties America,* by William Stott, and *The Dream and the Deal,* by Jerre Mangione. According to Stott, "emotion counted more than fact" in a documentary, a mode which had "pervasive influence...on the culture" in the 1930s. Two opposing forces influenced "documentary imagination"—the urge "to general experience" and "to affirm the intensely regional, the personal...." "*The Dream and the Deal* reads like a WPA guide itself—full of particulars, rich in characters and lore." Orvell refers to Conrad Aiken, Saul Bellow, John Cheever, Edward Dahlberg, Ralph Ellison, David Ignatow, Claude McKay, Harold Rosenberg, and Richard Wright as "already famous and yet-to-be-known writers who worked for the Federal Writers' Project.

363   Osofsky, Gilbert. "The Negro in New York: An Informal Social History." *New York Times Book Review,* 25 June 1967, p. 7.

364   Osofsky, Gilbert, ed. *Puttin' on Ole Massa.* New York, NY: Harper and Row, 1969.
       Includes a discussion of the significance of slave narratives.

365   Overmeyer, Grace. *Government and the Arts.* New York, NY: Norton, 1939.

366   Owens, Leslie Howard. *This Species of Property: Slave Life and Culture in the Old South.* New York, NY: Oxford University Press, 1976. 291 pp.

367   Papenfuse, Edward C. "A Modicum of Commitment: The Present and Future Importance of the Historical Records Survey." *American Archivist* 37:2 (April 1974): 211-221.
       Claims that the Historical Records Survey, originally a part of the Federal Writers' Project produced high quality work through the leadership of Luther Evans and the efficient work of his staff, many of whom were inexperienced workers.

368   Patterson, James T. "The New Deal and the States." *American Historical Review* 73 (October 1967): 70-84.

369   Pells, Richard H. *Radical Visions and American Dreams: Cul-
       ture and Social Thought in the Depression Years.* New York,
       NY: Harper and Row, 1973. 424 pp.

370   "Pen Project—America, the WPA, and 20,000,000 Words." *The
       Pathfinder,* 17 December 1938.

371   Penkower, Monty Noam. "The Federal Writers' Project: A Study
       in Government Patronage of the Arts." Ph.D. dissertation,
       Columbia University, 1970.

372   Penkower, Monty Noam. *The Federal Writers' Project: A Study
       in Government Patronage of the Arts.* Urbana, IL: University
       of Illinois Press, 1977. 266 pp.

373   Penrod, John A. "American Literature and the Great Depression."
       Ph.D. dissertation, University of Pennsylvania, 1954.

374   Perdue, Charles L., Jr. *Journal of American Folklore* 96 (Octo-
       ber-December 1983): 474-476.

       Review of *Toting the Lead Row: Ruby Pickens Tartt, Ala-
       bama Folklorist,* by Virginia Pounds Brown and Laurella
       Owens. [University, AL: University of Alabama Press, 1981.
       180 pp.]

375   Perdue, Charles L., Jr. "Old Jack and the New Deal: The Virginia
       Writers' Project and Jack Tale Collecting in Wise County,
       Virginia." *Appalachian Journal: A Regional Studies Review*
       [Boone, NC] 14:2 (Winter 1987): 108-152.

376   Perdue, Charles L., Jr., Thomas E. Barden, Robert K. Phillips,
       eds. *An Annotated Listing of Folklore Collected by Workers
       of the Virginia Writers' Project, Work Projects Administra-
       tion: Held in the Manuscripts Department at Alderman Li-
       brary of the University of Virginia.* Norwood, PA: Norwood
       Editions, 1979. 360 pp.

377   Perdue, Charles L., Jr., Thomas E. Barden, and Robert K. Phil-
       lips, eds. *Weevils in the Wheat: Interviews with Virginia
       Ex-Slaves.* Charlottesville, VA: University Press of Virginia,
       1976. 405 pp.

       Presents an important study of the Virginia Federal Writers'
       Project and its efforts to collect ex-slave narratives.

378   Phillips, Ulrich Bonnell. *American Negro Slavery.* New York,
       NY: D. Appleton-Century Co., 1940.

379   Pietan, Norman. "Federal Government and the Arts." Ph.D. dis-
       sertation, Columbia University, 1950.

380   Pittman, Dan W. "The Founding of Dyess Colony." *Arkansas Historical Quarterly* 29:4 (Winter 1970): 313-326.

381   Pitts, Walter. "Beyond Hypercorrection: The Use of Emphatic -*z* in BEV." *Chicago Linguistic Society*, pp. 303-310. Chicago, IL: Chicago Linguistic Society, 1981.

382   Pitts, Walter. "Contrastive Use of Verbal -*z* in the Slave Narratives." In *Diversity and Diachrony*, edited by David Sankoff, pp. 73-82. Amsterdam: John Benjamins, 1986.

383   Poplack, Shana and Sali Tagliamonte. "There's No Tense Like the Present: Verbal -*S* Inflection in Early Black English." In *The Emergence of Black English: Text and Commentary*, pp. 275-324, edited by Guy Bailey, Natalie Maynor, and Patricia Cukor-Avila. Amsterdam: John Benjamins, 1991.

       Refers to studies of the ex-slave narratives collected by the Federal Writers' Project.

384   Porter, David. "Senator Carl Hatch and the Hatch Act of 1939." *New Mexico History Review* 48 (1973): 151-164.

       Presents a study about the sponsor of the legislation who generally supported New Deal programs but was concerned about the political activities of the workers for the WPA.

385   Powell, Evanell K. *WPA Writers' Publications: A Complete Bibliographic Check List and Price Guide of Items, Major and Minor, of the Federal Writers' Project and Program.* Palm Beach, FL: Powell, 1970. 78 pp.

386   Powell-Brant, Evanell K. *WPA Federal Writers' Project, With Emphasis on the Florida Writers and Carita Doggett Corse.* Lake Panasoffkee, FL: E.K. Powell-Brant, 1990.

387   "Publishers' Letter on Federal Writers' Project." *Publishers Weekly*, 20 May 1939, 1817.

388   "Publishers' Letter on Federal Writers' Project." *Publishers Weekly*, 27 May 1939, 1919.

389   Putnam, Jared. "Guides to America." *Nation*, 24 December 1938, p. 694-696.

       Claims that the contents of the FWP guides "is amazingly rich and colorful, presented rather informally in a pleasing and always adequate manner. Not one of the books is dull." Notes that some of the spontaneity of the first books published has been lost in later volumes. States that the "hullabaloo against the Massachusetts book" for including material about the Sacco-Vanzetti case and labor relations led to the tendency in later books to follow a form so that material is "fitted by formula," to have books reviewed by a special policy editor in Washington, and to require all books to have state clearance. Reminds the reader that "the 'boondogglers' of the Federal Writers' Project would seem not to have had their feet on their desks all the time. Both the quality and quantity of their work are impressive."

390   Quinn, Patrick M. "Archivists and Historians: The Times They Are a Changin'." *Midwestern Archivist* 2:2 (1977): 5-13.

391   Rabson, Diane M. "Forty Years of Change: Contrasting Images of Lower Downtown Denver." *Colorado Heritage*, 4 (1983): 36-47.

392   Rader, Frank J. "Harry L. Hopkins, The Ambitious Crusader: An Historical Analysis of the Major Influences On His Care." *Annals of Iowa* 44:2 (1977): 83-102.

Discusses the influences of Hopkins' family, his education at Grinnell College, his career in social work, and political interests on his work as a relief administrator and as an assistant to the President during the war years.

393   Rader, Frank John. "Harry L. Hopkins: The Works Progress Administration and National Defense, 1935-1940." Ph.D. dissertation, University of Delaware, 1973.

394   Randall, Frederika. "New Deal New York." *Nation*, 15 January 1983, p. 52.

"In this generally enervating class of literature [travel and tourist guidebooks], the American Guide Series is a great eccentric," whose "striking feature" is "its perspective and sensibility [which] are more sophisticated than we expect from a guidebook today." Refers to the work of Richard Wright, Ralph Ellison, Claude McKay, David Ignatow, and Maxwell Bodenheim in this review of *The WPA Guide to New York City: The Federal Writers' Project Guide to 1930s New York*, with a new introduction by William H. Whyte. [New York, NY: Pantheon Books: 1983. 680 pp.]

395   Rapport, Leonard. "Comment." *Oral History Review* (1980): 89-92.

Consists of Rapport's concluding statement to the exchange with Tom Terrill and Jerrold Hirsch. [See "How Valid Are the Federal Writers' Project Life Stories: An Iconoclast Among the True Believers" and "Replies to Leonard Rapport's 'How Valid Are the Federal Writers' Project Life

Stories: An Iconoclast Among the True Believers.'"] Presents
a challenge to determine the validity of one particular story,
called a "seven dollar bill" story, through the "tedious method
of verification" or the more "cerebral" approach of the historian.

396   Rapport, Leonard. "How Valid Are the Federal Writers' Project
       Life Stories: An Iconoclast Among the True Believers." *Oral
       History Review* (1979): 6-17.

       Describes his experiences with the Writers' Project in North
       Carolina. Questions the authenticity, particularly the verbal
       accuracy, of many of the life stories collected and later
       published. Claims that writers, and those certified by relief
       agencies as writers, were not the best people to collect life
       stories because they were too likely to create stories rather
       than record them. Uses one story as an example of what "read
       then, as it reads now, like a seven-dollar bill."

397   Rauch, Basil. *The History of the New Deal 1933-1938.* New
       York, NY: Creative Age Press, 1944. 368 pp.

398   Rawick, George P., ed. *The American Slave: A Composite Auto-
       biography.* Contributions in Afro-American and African
       Studies, no. 11. 19 vols. Series 1 and 2. Westport, CT: Green-
       wood Publishing Company, 1972.

       Vol. 1: *From Sundown to Sunup: The Making of the Black
       Community,* by George P. Rawick. Vol. 2: *South Carolina
       Narratives, Parts I and II.* Vol. 3: *South Carolina Narratives,
       Parts III and IV.* Vol. 4: *Texas Narratives, Parts I and II.* Vol.
       5: *Texas Narratives, Parts III and IV.* Vol. 6: *Alabama and
       Indiana Narratives.* Vol. 7: *Oklahoma and Mississippi Nar-
       ratives.* Vol. 8: *Arkansas Narratives, Parts I and II.* Vol. 9:
       Arkansas Narratives, Parts III and IV. Vol. 10: *Arkansas
       Narratives, Parts V and VI.* Vol. 11: *Arkansas Narratives,
       Part VII, and Mississippi Narratives.* Vol. 12: *Georgia Nar-
       ratives, Parts I and II.* Vol. 13: *Georgia Narratives, Parts III
       and IV.* Vol. 14: *North Carolina Narratives, Part I.* Vol. 15:
       North Carolina Narratives, Part II. Vol. 16: *Kansas, Ken-
       tucky, Maryland, Ohio, Virginia, and Tennessee Narratives.*
       Vol. 17: *Florida Narratives.* Vol. 18: *Unwritten History of
       Slavery* (Fisk University). Vol. 19: *God Struck Me Dead* (Fisk
       University).

       The first volume stresses the importance of the slave narra-
       tives in demonstrating that the slaves developed a community

and resisted harsh treatment. The other volumes contain typescripts of the interviews collected by the Federal Writers'
Project and by Fisk University.

399   Rawick, George P., General Editor. Jan Hillegas, Ken Lawrence
       and Clarice T. Campbell, editors. *The American Slave: A
       Composite Autobiography.* Contributions to Afro-American
       and African Studies, no. 35. 12 vols. Supplement, Series 1.
       Westport, CT: Greenwood Press, 1977. 2412 pp.

       Vol. 1: *Alabama Narratives.* Vol. 2: *Arkansas, Colorado,
       Minnesota, Missouri and Oregon and Washington Narra-
       tives.* Vol. 3: *Georgia Narratives, Part I.* Vol. 4: *Georgia
       Narratives, Part II.* Vol. 5: *Indiana and Ohio Narratives.* Vol.
       6: *Mississippi Narratives, Part I.* Vol. 7: *Mississippi Narra-
       tives, Part II.* Vol. 8: *Mississippi Narratives, Part III.* Vol. 9:
       Mississippi Narratives, Part IV. Vol. 10: *Mississippi Narra-
       tives, Part V.* Vol. 11: *North Carolina and South Carolina
       Narratives.* Vol. 12: *Oklahoma Narratives.*

400   Rawick, George P., ed. *The American Slave: A Composite Auto-
       biography.* Contributions to Afro-American and African
       Studies, no. 49. 10 Vols. Supplement, Series 2. Westport, CT:
       Greenwood Press, 1979.

       Vol. 1: *Alabama, Arizona, Arkansas, District of Columbia,
       Florida, Georgia, Indiana, Kansas, Maryland, Nebraska,
       New York, North Carolina, Oklahoma, Rhode Island, South
       Carolina, Washington Narratives.* Vols. 2-10: *Texas Narra-
       tives.*

401   Reed, J. D. "Five Poems: The Reports Come In; WPA; The
       Weather Is Brought to You; Lost Silvertip; Pigs." *New
       Yorker,* 12 July 1969, p. 38.

402   *Register of the WPA Collection.* Salt Lake City, UT: Utah State
       Historical Society, 1979. 58 pp.

403   Richards, David. "Theater." *Washington Post,* 11 September
       1983, Section G, p. 1.

       Reports that Horizons, formerly the Pro Femina Theatre, will
       present *Woman's Work,* which is based on interviews col-
       lected by the Federal Writers' Project.

404   Ring, Daniel F. "The Cleveland Public Library and the WPA: A
       Study in Creative Partnership." *Ohio History* 84:3 (Summer
       1975): 158-164.

       Discusses the contributions of the Federal Writers' Project in
       providing jobs to produce The Annals of Cleveland, the

Union Catalogue, and the Historical Records Survey of Cuyahoga County.

405   Rohrs, Richard C. "The Study of Oklahoma History During the Territorial Period: An Alternative Methodological Approach." *Chronicles of Oklahoma* 60 (1982): 174-185.

406   Rosenberg, Bruce A. *The Folksongs of Virginia: A Checklist of the WPA Holdings, Alderman Library, University of Virginia.* Charlottesville, VA: University Press of Virginia, 1969. 145 pp.

407   Rosenberg, Harold. "Anyone Who Could Write English." *New Yorker*, 20 January 1973, pp. 99-102.

408   Rosenstone, Robert A. "The Federal (Mostly Non-) Writers' Project." *Reviews in American History* 6:3 (1978): 400-404.
       A review article about *The Federal Writers' Project: A Study in Government Patronage of the Arts*, by Monty Noam Penkower [Urbana, IL: University of Illinois Press, 1977].

409   Rosenzweig, Roy, Barbara Jones-Smith, Janet Schrader, Carolyn Mitchell, and Joan Haring, eds. *Government and the Arts in Thirties America: A Guide to Oral Histories and Other Research Materials.* Fairfax, VA: George Mason University Press, 1986. 329 pp.
       Includes extensive listing of oral history interview projects in the first part, a list of archival collections in the second part. Presents a very useful source of information about types of material available in libraries and historical archives throughout the country.

410   Roskolenko, Harry. *When I Was Last on Cherry Street.* New York, NY: Stein and Day, 1965.
       Deals with the writers' experiences with the Federal Writers' Project.

411   Rowland, Leonore. *The Romance of La Puente Rancho.* Includes excerpts from *La Puente Valley, Past and Present,* by Janet Powell and Dan N. Powell [of the W.P.A. Writers' Project]. Compiled and written by Leonore Rowland. Covina, CA: Neilson Press, 1958. 68 pp.

412   Rozwenc, Edwin Charles, ed. *The New Deal: Revolution or Evolution?* Revised edition, *Problems in American Civilization: Readings Selected by the Department of American Studies,* Amherst College. Boston, MA: D. C. Heath, 1959. 113 pp.

413   Rundell, Walter, Jr. "Main Trends in U.S. Historiography Since the New Deal: Research Prospects in Oral History." *Oral History Review* (1976): 35-47.

414   Ryan, Bonnie Crarey. "Zora Neale Hurston: A Checklist of Secondary Sources." *Bulletin of Bibliography* 45:1 (1988): 33-39.

Includes information about Hurston's work as as anthropologist and folklorist as well as literary criticism and book reviews.

415   Samuels, Peggy and Harold Samuels. "Frederic Remington, The Holiday Sheepman." *Kansas History* 2 (1979): 3-13.

Bases details about Remington as an unsuccessful sheep rancher and artist in Peabody, Kansas on WPA interviews with people who knew Remington in Kansas.

416   Sandberg, Elisabeth. "Jo Sinclair: Toward a Critical Biography." Ph.D. dissertation, University of Massachusetts, 1985.

Presents a critical biography of Jo Sinclair [Ruth Seid], a part of which looks at her early stories, "especially from her years on the WPA and with the Red Cross." Jo Sinclair received the Harper Prize for her first novel, *Wasteland.*

417   Saunders, D. A. "The Dies Committee, First Phase." *Public Opinion Quarterly* 3 (April 1939): 223-238.

Provides important background reading about the origin and purpose of the House Committee to Investigate Un-American Activities, the Martin Dies committee. Although originally set up to investigate the activities of Nazi agents in America, the Committee turned its attention to Communism. Parnell Thomas, a member of the Committee, "concentrated on the WPA, with particular reference to the Federal Arts Projects."

418   Scharf, Arthur. "Selected Publications of the WPA Federal Writers' Project and the Writers' Program." In *The Dream and the Deal: The Federal Writers' Project, 1935-1943*, pp. 375-396, by Jerre Mangione. Boston, MA: Little, Brown and Company, 1972. 416 pp.
Philadelphia, PA: University of Pennsylvania Press, 1983. 432 pp.

A very useful and informative listing of publications by the Federal Writers' Project. Includes a set of criteria and an extensive checklist of publications.

419   Schneider, Edgar W. *American Earlier Black English: Morphological and Syntactic Variables.* Tuscaloosa, AL: University of Alabama Press, 1989. 314 pp.

Examines 104 narratives from nine states, material from the large collection of ex-slave interviews collected in the 1930s by the Federal Writers' Project. Also examines the sound recordings of ex-slave interviews, made for the Archive of Folk Song in relation to the written narratives.

420   Schneider, Edgar W. *Morphologische und syntaktische Variablen im amerikanischen Early Black English.* Bamberger Beitraege zur Englischen Sprachwissenschaft, Band 10. Frankfurt am Main-Bern, Germany: Peter Lang, 1981.

Revised version published as *American Earlier Black English: Morphological and Syntactic Variables.* [Tuscaloosa, AL: University of Alabama Press, 1989.]

421   Schneider, Edgar Werner. "On the History of Black English in the USA: Some New Evidence." *English World-Wide* 3 (May 1982): 18-46.

Presents a linguistic analysis of the ex-slave narratives collected by the Federal Writers' Project in the 1930s.

422   Schneider, Edgar W. "The Origin of the Verbal *-s* in Black English." *American Speech* 58 (1983): 99-113.

Analyzes the concord and nonconcord uses of the third person, singular, present tense verbal inflection in the ex-slave narratives collected by the Federal Writers' Project in the 1930s.

423   Schurmann, Franz. "Is There Consensus for a New WPA Jobs Program?" *Los Angeles Daily Journal*, 2 November 1982, p. 4.

424   Seelye, John and Charles C. Alexander. *New England Quarterly.* 59:2 (June 1986): 267-269.

Review of *Remembering America: A Sampler of the WPA American Guide Series*, edited by Archie Hobson. [New York, NY: Columbia University Press, 1985. 391 pp.]

425   Seelye, John and Charles C. Alexander. *Ohio History* 95 (Winter/Spring 1986): 64-65.

Review of *Remembering America: A Sampler of the WPA American Guide Series*, edited by Archie Hobson. [New York, NY: Columbia University Press, 1985. 391 pp.]

426   "Shadows of an Era: The WPA Collection of Virginia Photo-
          graphs." *Virginia Cavalcade* 36 (1987): 128-135.

          Includes photographs that W. Lincoln Highton provided for
          the Virginia state guidebook.

427   Shopes, Linda. *International Journal of Oral History* 4 (Novem-
          ber 1983): 205-208.

          Review of *Up before Daylight: Life Histories from the Ala-
          bama Writers' Project, 1938-1939*, by James Seay Brown.
          [University, AL: University of Alabama Press, 1982. 261 pp.]

428   Simpson, Robert. "The Shout and Shouting in Slave Religion of
          the United States." *Southern Quarterly* [University of Ne-
          braska] 23:3 (Spring 1985): 34-47.

          Makes extensive use of the interviews with former slaves
          collected by the Federal Writers' Project in analyzing the
          "wide diversity in the fusion of European Protestant and
          African American traditions."

429   Sirevag, Torbjorn. *The Eclipse of the New Deal: And the Fall of
          Vice-President Wallace, 1944*. Modern American History.
          Robert E. Burke and Frank Freidel, Editors. New York, NY:
          Garland, 1985. 703 pp.

          Contains brief comments about WPA programs on pp. 306-
          308.

430   Siskind, Aaron. *Harlem Document: Photographs 1932-1940*.
          Foreword by Gordon Parks. Text from Federal Writers' Pro-
          ject, edited by Ann Banks. Providence, RI: Matrix Publica-
          tion, 1981. 79 pp.

          Revised edition: Siskind, Aaron. *Harlem: Photographs 1932-
          1940*. Foreword by Gordon Parks. Text from Federal
          Writers' Program edited by Ann Banks. Washington, DC:
          National Museum of American Art, 1990. 79 pp.

          Banks, Ann, ed. *Harlem, 1932-1940*. Foreword by Gordon
          Parks. Introduction by Maricia Battle. Photographs by
          Aaron Siskind. [Reprint of 1981 edition.] Washington,
          DC: Smithsonian, 1991. 80 pp. paper.

          Title page of 1990 edition states: "Accompanies an exhibition
          of the photographs organized by the National Museum of
          American Art, Smithsonian Institution, Merry A. Foresta,
          curator. Exhibition dates, November 22, 1990-March 17,
          1991." Documents Harlem with photographs and interviews
          collected by Ralph Ellison, Richard Wright, and Zora Neale
          Hurston, who worked for the Federal Writers' Project.

431 Sitkoff, Harvard, ed. *Fifty Years Later: The New Deal Evaluated.* 1st ed. Philadelphia, PA: Temple University Press, 1985. 240 pp.

Includes articles on cultural legacy, social welfare, race relations, politics, and economics. Authors include Alan Lawson, Robert H. Bremner, Richard Kirkendall, Thomas K. McCraw, Harvard Sitkoff, Susan Ware, Charles H. Trout, Arnold A. Offner, and William E. Leuchtenburg.

432 Sklar, Robert. *Journal of American History* 62 (September 1975): 460-461.

Review of *Roosevelt's Image Brokers: Poets, Playwrights and the Use of the Lincoln Symbol,* by Alfred Haworth Jones. [Port Washington, NY: Kennikat Press, 1974.]

433 Sloan, Raymond H. "The WPA Federal Writers' Project in Franklin County, Virginia, 1938-1939." *Folklore and Folklife in Virginia* 2 (1980-1981): 4-13.

434 Smith, Douglas L[loyd]. *The New Deal in the Urban South.* Baton Rouge, LA: Louisiana State University Press, 1988. 287 pp., 24 cm.

435 Smith, Geoffrey S. *To Save a Nation: American Countersubversives, the New Deal, and the Coming of World War II.* New York, NY: Basic Books, 1973. 244 pp.

436 Smith, Page. *Redeeming the Time: A People's History of the 1920's and the New Deal.* New York, NY: McGraw-Hill, 1986. 1205 pp.

437 Soapes, Thomas F. "The Federal Writers' Project Slave Interviews: Useful Data Or Misleading Source." *Oral History Review* 2 (1977): 33-38.

Stresses the importance of the slave interviews as a means by which the slaves could speak for themselves, a viewpoint important to historians. Reviews the positions of such scholars as John Blassingame, Eugene Genovese, George Rawick, and Norman Yetman.

438 *Southwestern Historical Quarterly* 91 (October 1987): 266-267.

Review of *The WPA Guide to Texas,* edited by Robert A. Calvert and Anne Hodges Morgan. Reprint ed. (original publ. 1940).

439 Stampp, Kenneth M. *The Peculiar Institution: Slavery in the Ante-Bellum South.* New York, NY: Alfred A. Knopf, 1956. 435 pp.

440   Stampp, Kenneth M. "Rebels and Sambos: The Search for the
        Negro's Personality in Slavery." *Journal of Southern History*
        37 (August 1971): 367-392.
        Notes that because the ex-slave narratives were collected
        "after slavery, we can seldom be sure that what they contain
        are true expressions of the slaves."

441   Stanford, Edward Barrett. *Library Extension Under the WPA: An
        Appraisal of an Experiment in Federal Aid.* Chicago, IL:
        University of Chicago Press, 1944. 284 pp.

442   Starling, Marion Wilson. "The Slave Narrative: Its Place in
        American Literary History." Ph.D. dissertation, New York
        University, 1946.
        Uses the Federal Writers' Project narratives as well as other
        narratives from university and library collections, claiming to
        have found many more narratives than were previously
        thought to exist. Compares the Federal Writers' Project nar-
        ratives to the antebellum published accounts of slaves. Claims
        that the Federal Writers' Project narratives are the "fifth
        avenue" to the study of narratives.

443   Stevens, Errol W. "The Federal Writers' Project Revisited: The
        Indiana Historical Society's New Guide to the State of Indi-
        ana." *Indiana Magazine of History* 76:2 (1980): 97-102.
        States that a new guidebook will be published for tourists.
        Discusses the contributions as well as the criticims of the
        FWP state guide book, *Indiana: A Guide to the Hoosier State.*

444   Stewart, Daniel Ogden. *Fighting Words.* Third Congress of
        American Writers. New York, NY: Harcourt, Brace and
        Company, 1940.
        Dedicated to the League of American Writers, this book
        includes comments by Benjamin Botkin, Kenneth Burke,
        Dashiell Hammett, Melville J. Herskovits, Langston Hughes,
        Alain Locke, Alan Lomax, and Dorothy Parker. In his lecture,
        "Creative Listening," Hyde Partnow explained how he went
        about the task of collecting folklore. Benjamin Botkin took
        folklore "out of the museum" and offered it to writers because
        "folklore is the stuff of literature."

445   Storr, Robert. *Art in America* 71:8 (September 1983): 13.
        Review of *The WPA Guide to New York City: The Federal
        Writers' Project Guide to 1930's New York,* by William H.
        Whyte [New York, NY: Pantheon Books, 1982], mainly of

interest for references to John Cheever, Richard Wright, Louis Lozowick, and Raphael Soyer.

446   Stott, William. *Documentary Expression and Thirties America.* New York, NY: Oxford University Press, 1973. 361 pp.

447   Stuckey, Sterling. "Through the Prism of Folklore: The Black Ethos in Slavery." In *The Debate Over Slavery: Stanley Elkins and His Critics,* edited by Ann J. Lane, pp. 245-268. Urbana, IL: University of Illinois Press, 1971. 378 pp.

448   Stuttaford, Genevieve. *Publishers Weekly,* 12 April 1985, p. 95. Review of *Remembering America: A Sampler of the WPA American Guide Series,* edited by Archie Hobson. [New York, NY: Columbia University Press, 1985. 391 pp.]

449   Sung, Carolyn Hoover. *Overview of WPA Federal Writers' Project Materials in the Archive of Folk Song.* Washington, DC: The Archive, 1972.

450   Susman, Warren, ed. *Culture and Commitment 1929-1945.* Introduction and Notes by George Braziller. New York, NY: G. Braziller, 1973. 372 pp.

451   Swados, Harvey, ed. *The American Writer and the Great Depression.* American Heritage Series. Leonard W. Levy and Alfred Young, editors. Indianapolis, IN: Bobbs-Merrill, 1966. 521 pp.

"In this temporary but fruitful symbiosis of bureaucrat and creative spirit (with hacks and has-beens thrown in for good measure), serious writers, as well as playwrights and painters, were enabled to carry on their own individual work with a degree of basic security, and the government was enabled to complete such valuable collective projects as the archives programs, the folklore volumes, and the immensely ambitious state guidebooks." This view of the Federal Writers' Project introduces this collection of writing about the depression, including works by Jack Conroy, Sherwood Anderson, John Steinbeck, Erskine Caldwell, James Agee, Theodore Roethke, James T. Farrell, Muriel Rukeyser, Edward Dahlberg, Edmund Wilson, Nelson Algren, Richard Wright, E. E. Cummings, and Marc Blitzstein.

452   Swain, Martha H. "'The Forgotten Woman': Ellen S. Woodward and Women's Relief in the New Deal." *Prologue* 15:4 (Winter 1983): 201-213.

453   Taber, Ronald W. "The Federal Writers' Project in the Pacific
        Northwest: A Case Study." Ph.D. dissertation, Washington
        State University, 1969.

454   Taber, Ronald W. "Vardis Fisher and the 'Idaho Guide': Preserv-
        ing Culture for the New Deal." *Pacific Northwest Quarterly*
        59:2 (1968): 68-76.

455   Taber, Ronald W. "Vardis Fisher of Idaho, March 31, 1895-
        1968." *Idaho Yesterdays* 12 (Fall 1968): 2.

456   Taber, Ronald W. "Writers on Relief: The Making of the Wash-
        ington Guide, 1935-1941." *Pacific Northwest Quarterly* 61:4
        (1970): 185-192.
        Discusses the problems and difficulties encountered in pro-
        ducing the Washington state guide, including policy issues
        and personality differences.

457   Terkel, Studs. *American Dreams, Lost and Found.* New York,
        NY: Pantheon Books, 1980. 470 pp.

458   Terkel, Studs. *Chicago.* New York, NY: Pantheon, 1986. 148 pp.
        Presents a nostalgic view of his experiences in Chicago,
        including race relations and WPA art.

459   Terkel, Studs. *Hard Times: An Oral History of the Great Depres-
        sion.* New York, NY: Pantheon, 1970.

460   Terkel, Studs. *Talking to Myself: A Memoir of My Times.* New
        York, NY: Pantheon Books, 1977. 316 pp.

461   Terrill, Tom E. "The Federal Writer's Project." *American His-
        torical Review* 83 (December 1978): 1360.

462   Terrill, Tom E. and Jerrold Hirsch. "Replies to Leonard Rapport's
        'How Valid Are the Federal Writers' Project Life Stories: An
        Iconoclast Among the True Believers.'" *Oral History Review*
        (1980): 81-92.
        Claims that Rapport's criticisms of the Federal Writers' Pro-
        ject's life stories are based on two issues: his "wrong-headed
        equation of verbal accuracy with authenticity" and "the over-
        all assessment of the life histories." Concludes that the life
        histories are important to understanding the Southern mill and
        farm workers. Claims that the "validity of these life histories
        will be determined by the skill with which scholars read them
        and the use they make of them."

463   Terrill, Tom and Jerrold Hirsch. "Such As Us." *Southern Expo-
        sure* 6:1 (1978): 67-72.

464   Terrill, Tom E. and Jerrold Hirsch, eds. *Such As Us: Southern Voices of the Thirties*. Chapel Hill, NC: University of North Carolina Press, 1978. 302 pp.

Includes life histories of Southern mill workers and farmers, collected in the Southeast by workers for the Federal Writers' Project.

465   "Their Own Baedeker." *New Yorker*, 20 April 1949, pp. 17-18.

466   Thomas, James W. "Lyle Saxon's Struggle with *Children of Strangers*." *Southern Studies* 16 (1977): 27-40.

Explains that his work with the Federal Writers' Project was one reason that Saxon took seven years to complete the novel. Notes that procrastination, socializing, and alcoholism also caused delay in finishing the novel.

467   Thomas, Joseph D. and Marsha McCabe, eds. Special issue of *Spinner: People and Culture in Southeastern Massachusetts*, Vol. 4, 1988. 234 pp.

Includes materials from the Federal Writer's Project as well as recent interviews to present a context for discussing the Federal Writers' Project in Massachusetts.

468   Thomson, Virgil. *A Virgil Thomson Reader*. Boston, MA: Houghton Mifflin, 1981.

Discusses the Federal Writers' Project in his autobiography.

469   Tierney, John. "A WPA for the Eighties." *Playboy*, April 1983, p. 129.

470   Tingley, Donald F. *Journal of the Illinois State Historical Society* 77:2 (Summer 1984): 147-148.

Review of *The WPA Guide to Illinois: The Federal Writers' Project Guide to the 1930s*, edited by Harris, Neil and Michael Conzen. Reprint ed. [originally published in 1939]. [New York, NY: Pantheon Books, 1933. 687 pp.]

471   Tomasi, Mari. "The Italian Story in Vermont." *Vermont History* 28:1 (January 1960).

472   Tomasi, Mari. *Like Lesser Gods*. Milwaukee, 1949.

A novel based on the experience of collecting granite industry narratives.

473   Touhey, Eleanor. "American Baedekers." *Library Journal*, 15 April 1941, pp. 339-341.

474   Traylor, Jack W. *History: Review of New Books* 11 (May-June 1983): 171.

Review of *Up before Daylight: Life Histories from the Alabama Writers' Project, 1938-1939*, by James Seay Brown.
[University, AL: University of Alabama Press, 1982. 261 pp.]

475   Turchen, Lesta VanDerWert. "Dakota Resources: Mss." *South
Dakota History* 11:3 (1981): 226.

Discusses the work of the Federal Writers' Project in South
Dakota with particular reference to the ex-slave narratives.

476   Tweton, D. Jerome. *The New Deal at the Grass Roots: Programs
For the People in Otter Tail County, Minnesota*. St. Paul, MN:
Minnesota Historical Society Press, 1988. 205 pp.

477   Tyler, Ronnie C. and Lawrence Murphy, eds. *The Slave Narratives of Texas*. Austin, TX: Encino Press, 1974. 143 pp.

The editors claim that the WPA ex-slave narratives are largely
unedited. Actually the narratives are extensively edited, making the volume useful only for gaining an idea of topics
included in the few narratives included.

478   Ulrich, Mabel. "Salvaging Culture for the WPA." *Harper's* 177
(May 1939): 653-654.

Recounts the problems of the Federal Writers' Project in
Minnesota. "Only when I was no longer permitted to do
honest and efficient work did I resign." Concludes that weak-
nesses of the WPA cultural programs should be corrected:
"lack of established standards of work" and "removal of the
cultural projects from the relief stipulation."

479   Umland, Rudolph. "On Editing WPA Guide Books." *Prairie
Schooner* 13 (Fall 1939): 160.

480   "Unemployed Arts." *Fortune* 15 (May 1937): 108-117.

"[The WPA programs] brought the American artist and the
American audience face to face for the first time in their
respective lives and the result was an astonishment needled
with excitement." Focuses on the performing arts.

481   "Unemployed Writers." *Saturday Review of Literature* 31 October 1936, p. 8.

482   United Press International. "Almanac 6." 26 April 1983.

Includes in the list of historical events for Friday, May 6, the
births of psychiatrist Sigmund Freud in 1856, Arctic explorer
Robert Peary in 1856, actor Rudolph Valentino in 1895, and
actor-director Orson Welles in 1915. Also, in 1935, the Works
Progress Administration, the WPA, was established to provide work for the unemployed during the Great Depression.

483   VanDeburg, William L. "Elite Slave Behavior During the Civil War: Black Drivers and Foremen in Historical Perspective." *Southern Studies* 16:3 (1977): 253-269.

484   VanDeburg, William L. "Slave Drivers and Slave Narratives: A New Look at the 'Dehumanized Elite.'" *Historian* 39 (1977): 717-732.

485   VanDeburg, William L. "The Slave Drivers of Arkansas: A New View from the Narratives." *Arkansas Historical Quarterly* 35 (1976): 231-245.

486   Vazzano, Frank P. "Harry Hopkins and Martin Davey: Federal Relief and Ohio Politics During the Great Depression." *Ohio History* 96 (Summer-Autumn 1987): 124-139.

487   Viereck, Wolfgang. "In Need of More Evidence on Black English: The Ex-Slave Narratives Revisited." In *Proceedings of the Society for Caribbean Linguistics*, ed. by Lawrence Carrington. Vol. 2, pp. 1-16. St. Augustine, Trinidad, West Indies: University of the West Indies, 1986.

488   Viereck, Wolfgang. "Invariant *Be* in an Unnoticed Source of American Early Black English." *American Speech* 63 (1988): 291-303.

       Discusses three sources of linguistic information about "'early' black English"—the Federal Writers' Project ex-slave narratives, the mechanically recorded interviews collected by the Archive of Folk Song, and the collection of 1,605 interviews collected and transcribed by Harry Middleton Hyatt. Analyzes the use of *be* and *be's* in the Hyatt collection and compares the findings with recent studies.

489   Viereck, Wolfgang, Edgar Schneider, and Manfred Goerlach. *A Bibliography of Writings on Varieties of English, 1965-1983.* Philadelphia, PA: John Benjamins, 1984.

490   Vincent, Charles. "Work Projects Administration Slave Narratives: A Biographical Resource for Both Slaves and Masters." *Journal of the Afro-American Historical and Genealogical Society* 9:2 (1988): 51-57.

       Notes that the more than 2,000 ex-slave narratives contain useful biographical information for the scholar, in spite of problems related to methodology and interviewing procedures.

491   Wade, Betsy. "Recalling Roots and Routes: The Work Projects Administration Guides Yield a Rich Harvest." *New York Times*, 3 Oct 1983, Section 10, p. 35.

Recognizes the contributions of the Federal Writers' Project travel guides. Refers to the work of Alexander L. Crosby, Vardis Fisher, and Jeremiah Digges.

492   Walker, Margaret. *Richard Wright: Daemonic Genius: A Portrait of the Man, a Critical Look at His Work.* New York, NY: Warner Books, 1988.

Notes that Richard Wright and Margaret Walker were friends when they both worked on the Chicago Federal Writers' Project in the 1930s. Presents information about his early years in rural Mississippi as well as the influences of Pan-Africanism, Marxism, his relationships with women, and his bohemian life in New York and Paris.

493   Waller, Charles T. *Georgia Historical Quarterly* 66 (Summer 1982): 268-269.

Review of *Toting the Lead Row: Ruby Pickens Tartt, Alabama Folklorist,* by Virginia Pounds Brown and Laurella Owens. [University, AL: University of Alabama Press, 1981. 180 pp.]

494   Walton, Eda Lou. "A Federal Writers' Anthology." *New York Times Book Review,* 29 August 1937, p. 2.

495   Ward, Geoffrey C. "The WPA Guide to New York, NY: The Federal Writers' Project Guide to 1930's New York." *Americana* 11:3 (July-August 1983): 64, 67.

496   Warren-Findley, Janelle. "Culture and the New Deal." *American Studies* [Lawrence, KS] 17:1 (1976): 81-83.

497   *Washington Post,* 31 March 1984, Section B, p. 6.

Obituary for Katharine Amend Kellock, an editor with the Works Projects Administration, who died on March 29 at age 91.

498   *Washington Post,* 2 August 1987, Book World, p. 12.

Review of *Remembering America: A Sampler of the WPA American Guide Series,* edited by Archie Hobson. [New York, NY: Columbia University Press, 1985. 391 pp.]

499   Wasser, Henry H. and Sigmund Skard, eds. "The New Deal and American Literature." In *Americana Norvegica: Norwegian Contributions to American Studies,* pp. 331-338. Oslo, Norway: Gyldendal Norsk, and Philadelphia, PA: University of Pennsylvania Press, 1966.

500   Waters, Thomas F. "The WPA Guide to the Minnesota Arrow-
        head Country. Federal Writers' Project." *Minnesota History*
        51 (Winter 1988): 158.

        Review of *The WPA Guide to the Minnesota Arrowhead
        Country,* reprint edition of 1941 edition. [St. Paul, MN:
        Minnesota Historical Society Press, 1988. 235 pp.]

501   Watkins, T[om] H. *Righteous Pilgrim: The Life and Times of
        Harold L. Ickes, 1874-1952.* New York: Henry Holt, 1990.
        1010 pp.

502   Watson, Alan D. "Review of North Carolina Nonfiction, 1978-
        1979." *North Carolina History Review* 57:2 (1980): 186-191.

        Review presented in the context of awarding the 1979 May-
        flower Cup. Paul D. Escott won the prize for his book, *Slavery
        Remembered: A Record of Twentieth-Century Slave Narra-
        tives.*

503   Webb, Constance. *Richard Wright: A Bibliography.* New York,
        NY: Putnam's, 1968.

504   Wechsler, James. "Record of the Boondogglers" [Part 1]. *Nation,*
        18 December 1937, pp. 680-683.

        Claims that in spite of "boondoggling" as an "inflammatory
        epithet for their activities...the fact is that in an atmosphere of
        distrust and humiliation WPA workers have fashioned a
        monumental record" of "enduring service...to the country."
        Starts this series of two articles by recounting the work
        accomplished in the first 13 months of the project, for exam-
        ple, building 29,000 miles of new roads, building 1,440
        recreational centers, building 1,099 new schools, and reno-
        vating 7,176 schools. Notes the "nation-wide experiment in
        adult education" was waging "a sweeping war on ignorance
        and illiteracy" by offering classes in 600 different subjects to
        more than 4,000,000 students.

505   Wechsler, James. "Record of the Boondogglers" [Part 2]. *Nation,*
        25 December 1937, pp. 715-717.

        Continues in this second article with a focus on the arts
        projects of the WPA, claiming that the record signifies the
        "dissolution of those barriers between the artist and the people
        which have caused American artists to stagnate in poverty and
        despair....WPA discovered an American audience, and that
        audience is being tutored," in art, in music, and in writing.
        Cites the FWP's extensive and impressive publication record
        with the guidebooks and related projects.

506   Wecter, Dixon. *The Age of the Great Depression, 1929-1941*. A History of American Life Series, Vol. 13. New York, NY: Macmillan, 1948. 362 pp.

Discusses the Federal Writers' Project as a new departure in federal government's approach to providing jobs. "Hacks, bohemians and eccentrics jostled elbows with highly trained specialists and creative artists of such past or future distinction as Conrad Aiken, Maxwell Bodenheim, Vardis Fisher, John Steinbeck, and Richard Wright.

507   Wecter, Dixon. *The Saga of American Society: A Record of Social Aspiration, 1607-1937*. New York, NY: Charles Scribner's Sons, 1937. 504 pp.

508   Weigle, Marta. "Finding the 'True America': Ethnic Tourism in New Mexico during the New Deal." *Folklife Annual* [Washington, DC] (1988-1989): 58-73.

509   Weinberger, Caspar. "Defense: Not a WPA." Letter. *Washington Post*, 15 March 1984, Section A, p. 20.

A letter about defense spending and the economic aspects of military policy. Refers to an earlier editorial, "Defense is Not the WPA" [27 February 1984].

510   Weisberger, Bernard A. "Federal Writers' Project, 1935-1943: The Legacy." *American Heritage* 25 (February 1974): 98.

511   Weisberger, Bernard A. "Reading, Writing, and History." *American Heritage* 25:2 (1974): 98-100.

512   Weisberger, Bernard A., ed. *The WPA Guide to America: The Best of 1930s America As Seen by the Federal Writers' Project*. Material originally written and compiled by the Federal Writers' Project of the Works Progress Administration. New York, NY: Pantheon Books, 1985. 462 pp.

513   Weisberger, Bernard. *The WPA Guide to America: New York*. New York, NY: Pantheon Books, 1985. 449 pp. paper.

514   Welge, William D. "Indian-Pioneer History Is 50 Years Old." *Chronicles of Oklahoma* 65 (1987): 319-321.

Discusses the Indian-Pioneer History Collection of interviews conducted with early Indian and white settlers in Oklahoma, a project directed by Grant Foreman.

515   Welsch, Roger L., ed. *Mister, You Got Yourself a Horse: Tales of Old-Time Horse Trading*. Lincoln, NE: University of Nebraska Press, 1981. 207p.

516 Welsch, Roger L. "Straight from the Horse Trader's Mouth." *Kansas Quarterly* 13:2 (1981): 17-26.

Based on horse trading stories collected by the Federal Writers' Project in Nebraska.

517 Welty, Eudora. "Looking Back at the First Story." *Georgia Review* 33:4 (1979): 741-755.

518 Wertheim, Arthur Frank. *History Teacher* 9 (February 1976): 327-328.

Review of *These Are Our Lives, As Told by the People and Written by Members of the Federal Writers' Project of the Works Progress Administration in North Carolina, Tennessee, Georgia*. Reprint edition of 1939 edition. [New York, NY: Norton, 1975. 421 pp.]

519 West, Hollie I. "The Teacher" [Sterling A. Brown]. *Washington Post*, 16 November 1969.

520 West, John O. "Jack Thorp and John Lomax: Oral Or Written Transmission?" *Western Folklore* 26:2 (1967): 113-118.

Claims that Lomax changed some texts and copied others, particularly from the cowboy songs of Jack Thorp. The claims are based on close textual study and analysis of the two collectors.

521 Westling, Louise. "The Loving Observer Of *One Time, One Place*." *Mississippi Quarterly*, 39:4 (Fall 1986): 587-604.

From 1934-1936, Eudora Welty worked as a photographer for the WPA. Her experiences as she traveled in Mississippi influenced her as a writer. In *One Time, One Place*, Welty published some of her photographs.

522 "What the Writers Wrote." *New Republic*, 1 September 1937, pp. 89-90.

Notes that the FWP has received less public attention than the other arts projects because the task of compiling information for books is "less spectacular that covering a wall with a mural or putting on a musical concert or a play." Recognizes the quality and quantity of publications by the FWP and claims that "on the whole, there has been a sympathetic effort to encourage creative writing...."

523 White, Graham J. and John Maze. *Harold Ickes of the New Deal: His Private Life and Public Career*. Cambridge, MA: Harvard University Press, 1985. 263 pp.

524   White, James P. "Government and Art: A New Deal Venture." *Markham Review* [Staten Island, NY] 4 (1975): 85-89.

525   Wideman, John Edgar. "Charles Chesnutt and the WPA Narratives: The Oral and Literate Roots of Afro-American Literature." In *The Slave's Narrative*, edited by Charles T. Davis, and Henry Louis Gates, Jr., pp. 59-78. Oxford, England: Oxford University Press, 1985. 342 pp.

       Notes that Chesnutt drew from both the literate and oral traditions, the "Anglo-Saxon literary tradition" and the "black oral tradition." Explains that Chesnutt uses an innovation for which he seldom receives credit—the use of a tale within a tale as a frame that "displays the written and spoken word on equal terms or at least as legitimate contenders for the reader's sympathy." Illustrates the technique with Chesnutt's story, "A Deep Sleeper," and with stories included in the slave narratives collected by the Federal Writers' Project.

526   Widner, Ronna Lee. "Lore for the Folk: Benjamin A. Botkin and the Development of Folklore Scholarship in America." *New York Folklore* 12:3-4 (1986): 1-22.

       Discusses Botkin's significant contributions to American folklore, including his work with the Federal Writers' Project.

527   Willis, William S. "Anthropology and Negroes on the Southern Cultural Frontier." In *The Black Experience in America*. Edited by James C. Curtis and Lewis L. Gould. Austin, TX: University ot Texas Press, 1970.

528   Wilson, Edmund. *The Thirties: From Notebooks and Diaries of the Period*. Edited with an introduction by Leon Edel. New York, NY: Farrar, Straus, and Giroux, 1980. 753 pp.

529   Winans, Robert B. "Sadday Night and Sunday Too: The Uses of Slave Songs in the WPA Ex-Slave Narratives for Historical Study" *New Jersey Folklore* 7 (Spring 1982): 10-15.

530   Winger, Howard W. *Library Quarterly* 53 (April 1983): 198.

       Review of *Pickaxe and Pencil: References for the Study of the WPA*, by Marguerite D. Bloxom. [Washington, DC: Library of Congress, 1982. 87 pp.]

531   Witt, Richard C. "The WPA Federal Writers' Project in Nebraska." M.A. Thesis, University of Nebraska at Lincoln, 1980. 160 pp.

532   Wolf, Edwin. *Pennsylvania Magazine of History and Biography* 114:1 (January 1990): 152-155.

Review of *The WPA Guide to Philadelphia,* compiled by the Federal Writers' Project. 2nd reprint edition. [Philadelphia, PA: University of Pennsylvania Press, 1988. 704 pp.]

533   Wolfram, Walt. "Re-Examining Vernacular Black English." *Language* 66 (1990): 121-133.

Review of *American Earlier Black English: Morphological and Syntactic Variables,* by Edgar W. Schneider [Tuscaloosa, AL: University of Alabama Press, 1989] and *The Death of Black English,* by Ronald R. Butters [Frankfurt am Main, Germany: Peter Lang, 1989. 227 pp.].

534   Wolfskill, George. *Pacific Northwest Quarterly* 66 (October 1975): 186.

Review of *Roosevelt's Image Brokers: Poets, Playwrights and the Use of the Lincoln Symbol,* by Alfred Haworth Jones. [Port Washington, NY: Kennikat Press, 1974.]

535   Wolfskill, George. *Happy Days Are Here Again!: A Short Interpretive History of the New Deal.* Berkshire Studies in History. Hinsdale, IL: Dryden Press, 1974. 226 pp.

536   Woodward, C. Vann. "History from Slave Sources." *American Historical Review* 79:2 (1974): 470-81.

Review of *The American Slave: A Composite Autobiography,* by George P. Rawick, General Editor [Westport, CT: Greenwood Publishing, 1972]. Focuses on the ex-slave interviews as historical sources. Concludes that the interviews are an important source of information from the slaves's point of view. Cautions that researchers should be aware of and prepared to deal with problems related to the use of the interviews as historical information, for example, the skewed sample and the biases of some of the interviewers.

537   Wooster, Martin Morse. "Bring Back the WPA? It Also Had a Seamy Side." *Wall Street Journal* 3 September 1986, p. 26.

"In the time of Franklin D. Roosevelt and that horrible Harry Hopkins, WPA stood for Works Progress Administration, and the purpose was to give jobs to people who were too feckless to find employment in private enterprise."

538   "Work of the FWP of the WPA." *Publishers Weekly,* 18 March 1939, pp. 1130-1135.

539   "WPA: It Wasn't All Just Leaf-raking." *Newsweek,* 20 January 1975, p. 57.

A one-page article arguing for a new WPA and explaining benefits of the old. Includes references to Elmer Rice, Studs Terkel, Nelson Algren, Richard Wright, and Saul Bellow.

540   *WPA Federal Writers' Project.* The Hofstra Library Associates Exhibition, "W.P.A.—The Writers' Project." Selected from the collection of Dr. Jen Yeh: November 8 to December 31, 1978. David Filderman Gallery, Hofstra Library. Hempstead, NY: Hofstra Library Associates, 1978. 23 pp.

541   "W.P.A. Folklore Collection." *California Folklore Quarterly* 3 (July 1944): 204-44.

        Briefly mentions that when the Southern California Writers' Project ended in 1942 many files were deposited with the University of California at Los Angeles.

542   "The WPA Guide to New York City." *New York Times Book Review*, 5 December 1982, Section 7, p. 54.

        Simply lists the book as a Christmas book.

543   "The WPA Guide to Washington, D.C." Review. *Southern Living* 19 (April 1984): 156.

544   "WPA, New-Style." *Nation*, 29 December 1962, p. 462.

        Claims that the WPA is one of the "residual ties between the glowing sixties and the gloomy thirties."

545   "WPA Writers Produce." *Publishers Weekly*, 21 August 1937, pp. 569-570.

546   "WPA Writers to Gather Municipal Data in 191 Cities." *American City* 52 (January 1937): 75.

        Reports that workers in the Federal Writers' Project would collect "comprehensive data on municipal governmental operations in 191 American cities," all cities "of more than 50,000 inhabitants."

547   "WPAccounting." *Time*, 15 February 1943, pp. 95-96.

        As the "last rites" were being said for the FWP, this article notes that the project's research and writing resulted in an "impressive job that will undoubtedly be valued for generations to come."

548   "Writers' Project: 1942." *New Republic*, 13 April 1942, p. 480.

        Describes the Federal Writers' Project Guide series as "the greatest writing and publishing venture of the decade....When we have won the fight against Hitler, which is also the fight for a free culture, the Writers' Project must be revived on a permanent basis."

549   Yardley, Jonathan. "Guiding Lights: Remembering America: A Sampler of the WPA American Guide Series." *Washington Post*, 22 May 1985, Section F, p. 2.

550   Yep, Laurence. *The Rainbow People*. Illustrated by David Wiesner. New York, NY: HarperCollins Children's Books, 1989. 208 pp.

Based on 20 Chinese folktales collected by the Federal Writers' Project in the Oakland Chinatown. A book for grade levels 3-7.

551   Yep, Laurence. *Tongues of Jade*. Illustrated by David Wiesner. New York, NY: HarperCollins Children's Books, 1991. 192 pp.

Based on early Chinese American folktales collected by the Federal Writers' Project in the Oakland Chinatown.

552   Yetman, Norman R. "The Background of the Slave Narrative Collection." *American Quarterly* 19:3 (Fall 1967): 534-53.

Discusses the characteristics of, the problems involved in studying, and the importance of the slave interviews collected by the Federal Writers' Project. Notes that the ex-slaves interviewed were over eighty years of age; the interviews were not selected randomly from the ex-slave population; the interviewers were typically untrained; the interviews were not recorded by tape recorder. Concludes that although the quality of the interview work was uneven, the "collection is an essential source of historical data."

553   Yetman, Norman R. "Ex-Slave Interviews and the Historiography of Slavery." *American Quarterly* 36:2 (Summer 1984): 181-210.

Discusses the importance of the collecting of the ex-slave interviews to the historiography of slavery in the U.S. Reviews four studies that make extensive use of the slave narratives: *Roll, Jordan, Roll*, by Eugene Genovese (1974), *The Black Family in Slavery and Freedom*, by Herbert Gutman (1976), *Slavery Remembered*, by Paul Escott (1979), and *Been in the Storm So Long*, by Leon Litwack (1979).

554   Yetman, Norman R., ed. *Life Under the "Peculiar Institution": Selections from the Slave Narrative Collection*. New York, NY: Holt, Rinehart and Winston, 1970.

555   Yetman, Norman R. "The Slave Personality: A Test of the 'Sambo' Hypothesis." Ph.D. dissertation, University of Pennsylvania, 1969.

556   Yetman, Norman R., ed. *Voices from Slavery.* New York, NY: Holt, Rinehart and Winston, 1970.
       This volume includes over 100 slave narratives from the WPA collection. Yetman chose narratives of slaves who were at least 13 years old at emancipation.

557   Yezierska, Anzia. *Red Ribbon on a White Horse.* New York, NY: Scribner's, 1950.
       Deals with the writer's experiences on the Federal Writers' Project.

558   Young, James S. *Black Writers of the Thirties.* Baton Rouge, LA: Louisiana State University Press, 1973. 257 pp.

559   Youngdale, James M. *North Dakota History* 53 (Winter 1986): 35.
       Review of *The WPA Guide to Minnesota*, compiled by the Federal Writers' Project Reprint ed. (original publ. 1938). [St. Paul, MN: Minnesota Historical Society, 1985. 539 pp.]

560   Zinn, Howard. *New Deal Thought.* The American Heritage Series. Indianapolis, IN: Bobbs-Merrill, 1966. 431 pp.

Section 2

Works by the Federal Writers' Project

State, City, and Local Guides,

Including Puerto Rico

Alabama

561   *Alabama: Collected Works of Federal Writers' Project.* Federal Writers' Project Staff. Irvine, CA: Reprint Services, 1991.

562   *Alabama: A Guide to the Deep South.* Compiled by workers of the Writers' Program of the Work Projects Administration in the State of Alabama. Sponsored by the Alabama State Planning Commission. New York: R. R. Smith, 1941. 442 pp.

Alaska

563   *A Guide to Alaska: Last American Frontier,* by Merle [Estes] Colby. Federal Writers' Project. New York: Macmillan Company, 1939. 427 pp.

Arizona

564   *Arizona: Collected Works of Federal Writers' Project.* Federal Writers' Project Staff. Irvine, CA: Reprint Services, 1991.

565   *Arizona: The Grand Canyon State: A State Guide.* Revised by Joseph Miller. Edited by Henry G. Alsberg and Harry Hansen. New York: Hastings House, 1966. 532 pp.

566   *Arizona: A State Guide.* Compiled by workers of the Writers' Program of the Work Projects Administration in the State of Arizona. Sponsored by the Arizona State Teachers College at Flagstaff. New York: Hastings House, 1940. 530 pp.
    The WPA Guide to 1930s Arizona. Original title: *Arizona: A State Guide.* Introduction by Stewart L. Udall. Tucson, AZ: University of Arizona Press, 1989. 530 pp. paper.

567   *Mission San Xavier del Bac, Arizona: A Descriptive and Histori-
        cal Guide.* Compiled by workers of the Writers' Program of
        the Work Projects Administration in the State of Arizona.
        Sponsored by Arizona Pioneers' Historical Society. New
        York: Hastings House, 1940. 57 pp.

Arkansas

568   *Arkansas: A Guide to the State.* Compiled by workers of the
        Writers' Program of the Works Projects Administration in the
        State of Arkansas. Sponsored by C. G. Hall, Secretary of
        State, Arkansas. New York: Hastings House, 1941. 447 pp.
        WPA Guide to 1930s Arkansas. Federal Writers' Project of the
        Works Progress Administration. Reprint of 1941 edition.
        Introduction by Elliott West. Lawrence, KS: University
        Press of Kansas, 1987. 512 pp. paper.

California

569   *Almanac for Thirty-Niners.* Palo Alto, CA: J. L. Delkin, 1938.
        127 pp.
570   *Balboa Park, San Diego, California: A Comprehensive Guide to
        the City's Cultural and Recreational Center.* San Diego, CA:
        Association of Balboa Park Institutions, 1941. 83 pp.
571   *California: Collected Works of Federal Writers' Project: North-
        ern Edition.* Federal Writers' Project Staff. Irvine, CA: Re-
        print Services, 1991.
572   *California: Collected Works of Federal Writers' Project: South-
        ern Edition.* Federal Writers' Project Staff. Irvine, CA: Re-
        print Services, 1991.
573   *California: A Guide to the Golden State.* Compiled and written
        by the Federal Writers' Project of the Works Progress Ad-
        ministration for the state of California. Sponsored by Mabel
        R. Gillis, California State Librarian. New York: Hastings
        House, 1939. 713 pp.
        Revised edition. New York: Hastings House, 1954. 716 pp.
        New revised edition. Harry Hansen, editor. New York: Hast-
        ings House, 1967. 733 pp.
        *The WPA Guide to California: The Federal Writers' Project
        Guide to 1930s California,* by the Federal Writers' Project
        Staff, Tillie Olsen, and Kenneth Patchen. Edited by Gwen-
        dolyn Wright. New York: Pantheon Books, 1984. 713 pp.
        paper.
574   *Death Valley: A Guide.* Written and compiled by the Federal
        Writer's Project of the Works Progress Administration of

northern California. Sponsored by the Bret Harte Associates. Boston, MA: Houghton Mifflin, 1939. 75 pp.

Revised edition. *Death Valley: The 1938 WPA Guide Updated for Today's Traveler.* Original title: *Death Valley.* Cheri Rae, editor. Preface by Ed Rothfuss. Santa Barbara, CA: Olympus Press, 1991. 160 pp. paper.

575   *Festivals in San Francisco.* Prepared by the Northern California Writers' Project of the Work Projects Administration. Sponsored by International Institute, Stanford University, and J.L. Delkin. San Francisco, CA: Grabhorn Press, 1939. 67 pp.

576   *A History of the Ranchos: The Spanish, Mexican, and American Occupation of San Diego and the Story of the Ownership of the Land Grants Therein,* by R. W. Brackett, with research and editorial supervision by the Federal Writers' Project of the Works Progress Administration, Southern California. Engravings on wood and cover design by Frank C. Barks. San Diego, CA: Union Title Insurance and Trust Company, 1939. 86 pp.

577   *The History of San Diego County Ranchos: The Spanish, Mexican, and American Occupation of San Diego County and the Story of the Ownership of Land Grants Therein.* 5th edition. San Diego, CA: Union Title Insurance and Trust Co., [1960]. 70 pp.

578   *Los Angeles: A Guide to the City and Its Environs.* Compiled by workers of the Writers' Program of Work Projects Administration in southern California. Sponsored by the Los Angeles County Board of Supervisors. New York: Hastings House, 1941. 433 pp.

2nd edition, completely revised. New York: Hastings House, 1951. 441 pp.

579   *Monterey Peninsula.* Compiled by workers of the Writers' Program of the Work Projects Administration in northern California. Sponsored by California State Department of Education. Stanford, CA: J.L. Delkin, 1941. 207 pp.

2nd revised edition. American Centennial Edition. Stanford, CA: J. L. Delkin, 1946. 200 pp.

WPA Guide to the Monterey Peninsula. Work Projects Administration Staff. Introduction by Page Stegner. Tuscon, AZ: University of Arizona Press, 1989. Reprint of 1946 edition. 247 pp. paper.

580   *Roads and Trails in the Vicinity of Mt. Tamalpais, Marin County, California: January, 1937.* Compiled by the Federal Writers'

Project of the Works Progress Administration. Map 82 x 85 cm. Federal Writers' Project, 1937.

581   *San Diego: A California City.* Prepared by the San Diego Federal Writers' Project. San Diego, CA: San Diego Historical Society, 1937. 138 pp.

582   *San Francisco: A Guide to the Bay and Its Cities.* Compiled by workers of the Writer's Program of the Work Projects Administration in northern California. Sponsored by the City and County of San Francisco. New York: Hastings House, 1940. 531 pp.

2nd edition, revised. New York: Hastings House, 1947. 531 pp.

New revised edition. Edited by Gladys Hansen. New York: Hastings House, 1973. 496 pp.

583   *Santa Barbara: A Guide to the Channel City and Its Environs.* Compiled and written by the Southern California Writers' Project of the Work Projects Administration. Sponsored by Santa Barbara State College. New York: Hastings House, 1941. 206 pp.

Colorado

584   *Colorado.* Northport, NY: Bacon & Wieck, 1940. 40 pp.

585   *Colorado: A Guide to the Highest State.* Compiled by workers of the Writers' Program of the Work Projects Administration in the state of Colorado. Sponsored by the Colorado State Planning Commission. New York: Hastings House, 1941. 511 pp.

New revised edition: Harry Hansen, editor. New York: Hastings House, 1970. 504 pp.

Reprint. *The WPA Guide to 1930s Colorado.* Federal Writers' Project of the Works Progress Administration. Introduction by Tom Noel. Lawrence, KS: University Press of Kansas, 1987. 576 pp. paper.

586   *Ghost Towns of Colorado.* Sponsored by Ralph L. Carr, Governor of Colorado. New York: Hastings House, 1947. 114 pp.

587   *Life in Denver.* Compiled by Colorado Writers' Program of the Work Projects Administration for use in Denver junior high schools. Sponsored by Department of Instruction, Denver Public Schools. Part I: "A Short History of Denver." Part II: "Government in Denver and Colorado." Part III: "Welfare and Social Service in Denver." Part IV: "Public Utilities in Denver." Part V: "Religion in Denver." Denver, CO: Denver Public Schools, Department of Instruction, 1940-1941. Mimeographed.

Connecticut

588   *Connecticut: Collected Works of Federal Writers' Project.* Federal Writers' Project Staff. Irvine, CA: Reprint Services, 1991.

589   *Connecticut: A Guide to Its Roads, Lore, and People.* Written by workers of the Federal Writers' Project of the Works Progress Administration for the State of Connecticut. Sponsored by Wilbur L. Cross. Boston, MA: Houghton Mifflin Company, 1938. 593 pp.

590   *History of Milford, Connecticut, 1639-1939.* Federal Writers' Project of Connecticut. Bridgeport, CT: Press of Braunworth & Co., Inc., 1939. 204 pp.

Delaware

591   *Delaware: Collected Works of Federal Writers' Project.* Federal Writers' Project Staff. Irvine, CA: Reprint Services, 1991.

592   *Delaware: A Guide to the First State.* Compiled and written by the Federal Writers' Project of the Works Progress Administration for the State of Delaware. Sponsored by Edward W. Cooch, Lieutenant Governor. New York: Viking Press, 1938. 549 pp.

     New and revised edition by Jeannette Eckman. Edited by Henry G. Alsberg. New York: Hastings House, 1955. 562 pp.

593   *New Castle on the Delaware.* Compiled by the Delaware Federal Writers' Project of the Works Progress Administration. Sponsored and published by the New Castle Historical Society. New Castle, DE: New Castle Historical Society, 1936. 142 pp.

     Reprint. Wilmington, DE: Press of W. N. Cann, Incorporated, 1937. 142 pp.

Florida

594   *Florida: Collected Works of Federal Writers' Project.* 2 volumes. Federal Writers' Project Staff. Irvine, CA: Reprint Services, 1991.

595   *Florida: A Guide to the Southern-Most State.* Compiled and written by the Federal Writers' Project of the Work Projects Administration for the State of Florida. Sponsored by State of Florida Department of Public Instruction. New York: Oxford University Press, 1939. 600 pp.

The WPA Guide to Florida. Introduction by Federal Writers'
Project Staff. New York: Pantheon, 1984.

596   *A Guide to Key West*. Compiled by workers of the Writers'
Program of the Work Projects Administration in the State of
Florida. New York: Hastings House, 1941. 122 pp.

597   *Miami and Dade County, Including Miami Beach and Coral
Gables*. Compiled by workers of the Writers' Program of the
Work Projects Administration in the State of Florida. Spon-
sored by the Florida State Planning Board. Northport, NY:
Bacon, Percy and Daggett, 1941. 202 pp.

Planning Your Vacation in Florida occurs at the head of the
title. The cover title is *Guide to Miami and Environs*.

598   *Seeing Fernandina: A Guide to the City and Its Industries*.
Compiled by workers of the Writers' Program of the Work
Projects Administration in the State of Florida. Sponsored by
the Florida State Planning Board. Fernandina, FL: Fernandian
News Publishing Company, 1940. 84 pp.

599   *Seeing St. Augustine*. Compiled and written by the Federal Writers' Project of the Works Progress Administration. Sponsored
by City Commission of St. Augustine. St. Augustine, FL: The
Record Company, 1937. 73 pp.

600   *The Spanish Missions of Florida*. St. Augustine, 1940. 51 pp.

Georgia

601   *Atlanta: Capital of the South*. Georgia Writers' Project. Edited
by Paul W. Miller. New York: O. Durrell, 1949. 318 pp.

602   *Atlanta: A City of the Modern South*. Georgia Writers' Project.
Compiled by workers of the Writers' Program of the Work
Projects Administration in the State of Georgia. Sponsored
by the Board of Education of the City of Atlanta. New York:
Smith and Durrell, 1942. 266 pp.

603   *Augusta*. Compiled and written by Augusta Unit, Federal Writers' Project in Georgia of the Works Progress Administration.
Augusta, GA: Tidwell Printing Supply Co., 1938. 218 pp.

604   *Georgia: Collected Works of Federal Writers' Project*. 2 volumes. Federal Writers' Project Staff. Irvine, CA: Reprint
Services, 1991.

605   *Georgia: A Guide to Its Towns and Countryside*. Compiled and
written by workers of the Writers' Program of the Work
Projects Administration in the State of Georgia. Sponsored
by the Georgia Board of Education. Athens, GA: University
of Georgia Press, 1940. 559 pp.

Revised and extended by George G. Leckie. Foreword by Ralph McGill. Atlanta, GA: Tupper and Love, 1954. 457 pp.

Introduction by Phinizy Spalding. Columbia, SC: University of South Carolina Press, 1990. 578 pp.

606 *The Macon Guide and Ocmulgee National Monument.* Compiled by workers of the Writers' Program of the Work Projects Administration in the State of Georgia. Sponsored by Macon Junior Chamber of Commerce. Macon, GA: J. W. Burke Co., 1939. 127 pp.

607 *Savannah.* Compiled and written by Savannah Unit, Federal Writers' Project in Georgia, Works Progress Administration. Savannah, GA: Review Printing Co., 1937. 108 pp.

608 *Savannah River Plantations*, by Savannah Writers' Project. Edited by Mary Granger. Savannah, GA: Savannah, Georgia Historical Society, 1947. 475 pp.

609 *The Story of Washington-Wilkes.* Compiled and written by workers of the Writers' Program of the Work Projects Administration in the State of Georgia. Sponsored by the Washington City Council. Athens, GA: University of Georgia Press, 1941. 136 pp.

Idaho

610 *Idaho: Collected Works of Federal Writers' Project.* Federal Writers' Project Staff. Irvine, CA: Reprint Services, 1991.

611 *Idaho: A Guide in Word and Picture.* Prepared by the Federal Writers' Project of the Works Progress Administration. Library edition. Caldwell, ID: Caxton Printers, 1937. 431 pp.

2nd edition revised. New York: Oxford University Press, 1950. 300 pp.

612 *The Idaho Encyclopedia.* Compiled by the Federal Writers' Project of the Works Progress Administration. Vardis Fisher, State Director. Caldwell, ID: Caxton Printers, Ltd., 1938. 452 pp.

613 *Idaho Lore.* Caldwell, ID: Caxton Printers, 1939. 256 pp.

Illinois

614 *Better Illinois Communities Through W.P.A. Projects.* Springfield, IL: Information Service, Works Progress Administration, Illinois, 1936. 31 pp.

615   *Du Page County: A Descriptive and Historical Guide, 1831-
       1939*. Federal Writers' Project of Illinois. Edited by Marion
       Knoblauch. Elmhurst, IL: I. A. Ruby, 1948. 253 pp.
          Revised edition. Edited by Marion Knoblauch. Wheaton, IL:
          Du Page Title Co., 1951. 253 pp.
616   *Galena Guide*. Federal Writers' Project of Illinois. Chicago, IL,
       1937.
617   *Illinois: Collected Works of Federal Writers' Project*. 2 volumes.
       Federal Writers' Project Staff. Irvine, CA: Reprint Services,
       1991.
618   *Illinois: A Descriptive and Historical Guide*. Compiled and
       written by the Federal Writers' Project of the Work Projects
       Administration for the State of Illinois. Sponsored by Henry
       Horner, Governor. Chicago, IL: A. C. McClurg and Co.,
       1939. 687 pp.
          St. Clair Shores, MI: Somerset Publishers, 1973. 687 pp.
          *The WPA Guide to Illinois: The Federal Writers' Project
          Guide to 1930s Illinois*. Federal Writers' Project. Edited
          by Neil Harris and Michael Conzen. New York: Pantheon
          Books, 1983. 687 pp.
619   *Nauvoo Guide*. Compiled and written by Federal Writers' Project
       of Illinois, Works Progress Administration. Chicago, IL: A.
       C. McClurg, 1939. 49 pp.
620   *Princeton Guide*. Compiled by the Federal Writers' Project of
       Illinois. Princeton, IL: Republican Printing Company, 1939.
       48 pp.

Indiana
621   *Indiana: Collected Works of Federal Writers' Project*. Federal
       Writers' Project Staff. Irvine, CA: Reprint Services, 1991.
622   *Indiana: A Guide to the Hoosier State*. Compiled by workers of
       the Writers' Program of the Work Projects Administration in
       the State of Indiana. Sponsored by the Department of Public
       Relations of Indiana State Teachers College. New York:
       Oxford University Press, 1941. 548 pp.

Iowa
623   *A Guide to Burlington, Iowa*. Compiled and written by the
       Federal Writers' Project of the Works Progress Administra-
       tion in the State of Iowa. Burlington, IA: Acres-Blackmar Co.,
       1938. 72 pp.

2d ed. Compiled and written by the Federal Writers' Project of the Works Progress Administration, State of Iowa. Burlington, IA: Acres-Blackmar Co., 1939. 80 pp.

624 *Guide to Cedar Rapids and Northeast Iowa.* Prepared by the Federal Writers' Project of Iowa. Cedar Rapids, IA: Laurence Press, 1937. 79 pp.

625 *A Guide to Dubuque.* Compiled and written by the Federal Writers' Project of the Works Progress Administration in the State of Iowa. Sponsored by the City of Dubuque and the Dubuque Chamber of Commerce. Dubuque, IA: Hoermann Press, 1937. 32 pp.

626 *A Guide to Estherville, Iowa, Emmet County, and Iowa Great Lakes Region.* Compiled and written by the Federal Writers' Project of the Works Progress Administration, State of Iowa. Sponsored by the Estherville Chamber of Commerce. Estherville, IA: Estherville Enterprise Print, 1939. 36 pp.

627 *Iowa: Collected Works of Federal Writers' Project.* Federal Writers' Project Staff. Irvine, CA: Reprint Services, 1991.

628 *Iowa: A Guide to the Hawkeye State.* Compiled and written by the Federal Writers' Project of the Works Progress Administration for the State of Iowa. Sponsored by the State Historical Society of Iowa to commemorate the Centenary of the organization of Iowa territory. New York: Viking Press, 1938. 538 pp.
Reprint edition. New York: Hastings House, 1940.
The WPA Guide to 1930s Iowa. Originally published as *Iowa: A Guide to the Hawkeye State,* 1938. Federal Writers' Project. Ames, IA: Iowa State University Press, 1986. 583 pp.

Kansas

629 *A Guide to Salina, Kansas.* Federal Writers' Project. Salina, KS: Advertiser-Sun, 1939. 55 pp.

630 *Kansas: Collected Works of Federal Writers' Project.* Federal Writers' Project Staff. Irvine, CA: Reprint Services, 1991.

631 *Kansas: A Guide to the Sunflower State.* Compiled and written by the Federal Writers' Project of the Work Projects Administration for the State of Kansas. Sponsored by State Department of Education. New York: Viking Press, 1939. 538 pp.
Reprint. *The WPA Guide to 1930s Kansas.* Original title, *Kansas: A Guide to the Sunflower State.* Introduction by James R. Sairtridge. Lawrence, KS: University Press of Kansas, 1984. 540 pp. paper.

Kentucky

632   *A Centennial History of the University of Louisville.* Louisville,
        KY: University of Louisville, 1939. 301 pp.

633   *Henderson: A Guide to Audubon's Home Town in Kentucky.*
        Compiled by workers of the Writers' Program of the Work
        Projects Administration in the State of Kentucky. Sponsored
        by Susan Starling Towles, librarian, Public Library, Hender-
        son, Kentucky. Northport, N Y: Bacon, Percy and Daggett,
        1941. 120 pp.

634   *In the Land of Breathitt.* Compiled by workers of the Writers'
        Program of the Work Projects Administration in the State of
        Kentucky. Northport, NY: Bacon, Percy and Daggett, 1941.
        165 pp.

635   *Kentucky: Collected Works of Federal Writers' Project.* Federal
        Writers' Project Staff. Irvine, CA: Reprint Services, 1991.

636   *Kentucky: A Guide to the Bluegrass State.* Compiled and written
        by the Federal Writers' Project of the Work Projects Admini-
        stration for the State of Kentucky. Sponsored by the Univer-
        sity of Kentucky. New York: Harcourt, Brace and Company,
        1939. 489 pp.
        Revised edition. New York: Hastings House, 1954. 402 pp.

637   *Lexington and the Bluegrass Country.* Written by workers of the
        Federal Writers' Project of the Works Progress Administra-
        tion. Lexington, KY: E. M. Glass, 1938. 149 pp.

638   *Louisville: A Guide to the Falls City.* Compiled by workers of the
        Writers' Program of the Work Projects Administration in the
        State of Kentucky. Sponsored by the University of Kentucky.
        Co-operating sponsor, the Louisville Automobile Club. New
        York: M. Barrows and Company, Inc., 1940. 112 pp.

639   *Old Capitol and Frankfort Guide.* Compiled and written by the
        Federal Writers' Project of the Works Progress Administra-
        tion. Frankfort, KY: H. McChesney, 1939. 98 pp.

640   *Union County, Past and Present.* Compiled by workers of the
        Kentucky Writers' Project of the Work Projects Administra-
        tion. Sponsored by the Union County Fiscal Court. Louisville,
        KY: Schuhmann Printing, 1941. 245 pp.

Louisiana

641   *Louisiana: Collected Works of Federal Writers' Project.* Federal
        Writers' Project Staff. Irvine, CA: Reprint Services, 1991.

642 *Louisiana: A Guide to the State.* Compiled by workers of the Writers' Program of the Work Projects Administration in the State of Louisiana. Sponsored by the Louisiana Library Commission at Baton Rouge. New York: Hastings House, 1941. 746 pp.

643 *New Orleans City Guide.* Written and compiled by the Federal Writers' Project of the Works Progress Administration for the City of New Orleans. Boston, MA: Houghton Mifflin Company, 1938. 430 pp.

Revised edition, by Robert Tallant. Boston, MA: Houghton Mifflin, 1952. 416 pp.

New York: Pantheon Books, 1983. 430 pp.

Maine

644 *Augusta-Hallowell on the Kennebec.* Compiled by workers of the Writers' Program of the Work Projects Administration in Maine. Augusta, ME: Kennebec Journal Print Shop, 1940. 123 pp.

645 *Maine: Collected Works of Federal Writers' Project.* Federal Writers' Project Staff. Irvine, CA: Reprint Services, 1991.

646 *Maine: A Guide "Down East."* Written by workers of the Federal Writers' Project of the Works Progress Administration. Boston, MA: Houghton Mifflin, 1937. 476 pp.

Maine: A Guide to the Vacation State, edited by Ray Bearse. 2nd edition, revised, of *Maine: A Guide "Down East."* Boston, MA: Houghton Mifflin, 1969. 460 pp.

Maine League of Historical Societies and Museums. 2nd edition. Edited by Dorris A. Isaacson. Rockland, ME: Courier-Gazette, 1970. 510 pp.

647 *Maine's Capitol.* Written and compiled by the Federal Writers' Project of the Work Projects Administration for the State of Maine. Augusta, ME: Kennebec Journal Print Shop, 1939. 60 pp.

648 *Portland City Guide.* Compiled by workers of Writers' Program of the Work Projects Administration in the State of Maine. Sponsored by the City of Portland. Portland, ME: Forest City Printing Company, 1940. 337 pp.

Maryland

649 *A Guide to the United States Naval Academy.* New York: Devin-Adair, 1941. 158 pp.

650 *Maryland: Collected Works of Federal Writers' Project.* Federal Writers' Project Staff. Irvine, CA: Reprint Services, 1991.

651   *Maryland: A Guide to the Old Line State.* Compiled by workers
        of the Writers' Program of the Work Projects Administration
        in the State of Maryland. Sponsored by Herbert R. O'Conor,
        Governor of Maryland. New York: Oxford University Press,
        1940. 561 pp.

Massachusetts

652   *An Almanack for Bostonians, 1939.* Federal Writers' Project of
        Massachusetts. New York, NY: M. Barrows and Company,
        1938.
653   *The Berkshire Hills.* Compiled and written by members of the
        Federal Writers' Project of the Works Progress Administra-
        tion for Massachusetts. Sponsored by the Berkshire Hills
        Conference, Inc. New York: Funk and Wagnalls, 1939.
        368 pp.
654   *The Berkshires: Collected Works of Federal Writers' Project.*
        Federal Writers' Project Staff. Irvine, CA: Reprint Services,
        1991.
655   *Boston: Collected Works of Federal Writers' Project.* Federal
        Writers' Project Staff. Irvine, CA: Reprint Services, 1991.
656   *Boston Looks Seaward: The Story of the Port, 1630-1940.* Edited
        by workers of the Writers' program of the Work Projects
        Administration in the State of Massachusetts. Sponsored by
        the Boston Port Authority. Boston, MA: B. Humphries, 1941.
        316 pp.
657   *A Brief History of the Towne of Sudbury in Massachusetts.*
        Sudbury, MA, 1939. 64 pp.
658   *Fairhaven, Massachusetts.* Fairhaven, MA, 1939. 60 pp.
659   *A Historical Sketch of Auburn, Massachusetts.* Federal Writers'
        Project of Massachusetts. Worcester, MA: Charles D. Cady
        Printing Co., 1937. 63 pp.
660   *Massachusetts: Collected Works of Federal Writers' Project.*
        Federal Writers' Project Staff. Irvine, CA: Reprint Services,
        1991.
661   *Massachusetts: A Guide to Its Places and People.* Written and
        compiled by the Federal Writers' Projects of the Works
        Progress Administration for the State of Massachusetts. Bos-
        ton, MA: Houghton Mifflin Company, 1937. 675 pp.
            2nd edition, revised. *Massachusetts: A Guide to the Pilgrim
            State,* edited by Ray Bearse. Boston, MA: Houghton Mif-
            flin, 1971. 525 pp.

Reprint. *The WPA Guide to Massachusetts: The Federal Writers' Project Guide to 1930s Massachusetts.* New York: Pantheon Books, 1983. 674 pp.

662 *State Forests and Parks of Massachusetts: A Recreation Guide.* Compiled and written by the Massachusetts WPA Federal Writers' Project. Boston, MA: Department of Conservation, 1941. 58 pp.

663 *Winter Sports and Recreation in the Berkshire Hills.* Compiled by workers of the Federal Writers' Project of the Works Progress Administration of Massachusetts. Pittsfield, MA, 1937.

Michigan

664 *Michigan: Collected Works of Federal Writers' Project.* Federal Writers' Project Staff. Irvine, CA: Reprint Services, 1991.

665 *Northwestern High School, 1914-1939, A History.* Federal Writers' Project, Michigan. Detroit: Goodwill Printing Co., 1939. 109 pp.

Minnesota

666 *The Mayors of St. Paul, 1850-1940, Including the First Three Town Presidents.* St. Paul: St. Paul Vocational School, 1940. 73 pp.

667 *Minneapolis: The Story of a City.* Minneapolis, 1940. 94 pp.

668 *Minnesota: Collected Works of Federal Writers' Project.* Federal Writers' Project Staff. Irvine, CA: Reprint Services, 1991.

669 *Minnesota: A State Guide.* Compiled and written by the Federal Writers' Project of the Works Progress Administration in the State of Minnesota. Sponsored by the Executive Council, State of Minnesota. New York: The Viking Press, 1938. 523 pp.

Revised edition. New York: Hastings House, 1954. 545 pp.

The WPA Guide to Minnesota. Federal Writers' Project. Introduction by Fredrick Manfred. Irvine, CA: Borealis Books, Reprint Series, Minnesota History, 1985. 539 pp. paper.

670 *The Minnesota Arrowhead Country.* Chicago, IL: A. Whitman, 1941. 231 pp.

Reprint. *The WPA Guide to the Minnesota Arrowhead Country.* Introduction by Francis M. Carroll. St. Paul: Minnesota Historical Society Press, 1988. 235 pp.

Mississippi

671   *Mississippi: A Guide to the Magnolia State.* Compiled and written by the Federal Writers' Project of the Works Progress Administration in Mississippi. New York: Viking, 1938. 545 pp.
        Reprint. New York: Hastings House, 1949. 545 pp.
        Reprint. Introduction by Robert McElvaine. Golden Anniversary Edition. Jackson, MS: University Press of Mississippi, 1988. 545 pp.
672   *Mississippi Gulf Coast, Yesterday and Today, 1699-1939.* Federal Writers' Project of Mississippi. Gulfport, MS: Gulfport Printing Co., 1939. 162 pp.

Missouri

673   *Missouri: A Guide to the "Show Me" State.* Writers' Program of the Work Projects Administration in the State of Missouri. Sponsored by the Missouri State Highway Department. New York: Duell, Sloan and Pearce, 1941. 652 pp.
        The WPA Guide to 1930s Missouri. Foreword by Charles Van Ravenswaay. Introduction by Howard Marshall. Introduction by Walter Schroeder. Lawrence, KS: University Press of Kansas, 1986. 656 pp. paper.
        The WPA Guide to 1930s Missouri. Lawrence, KS: University Press of Kansas, 1987. 652 pp

Montana

674   *Copper Camp: Stories of the World's Greatest Mining Town, Butte, Montana.* New York: Hastings House, 1943. 308 pp.
675   *Montana: Collected Works of Federal Writers' Project.* Federal Writers' Project Staff. Irvine, CA: Reprint Services, 1991.
676   *Montana: A State Guide Book.* Compiled and written by the Federal Writers' Project of the Work Projects Administration for the State of Montana. Sponsored by Department of Agriculture, Labor and Industry, State of Montana. New York: Viking Press, 1939. 430 pp.
        Revised edition. New York: Hastings House, 1955.

Nebraska

677   *Almanac for Nebraskans, 1939.* Prepared by the Federal Writers' Project of Nebraska. Lincoln, NE: Woodruff Printing Company, 1938.

678   *Lincoln City Guide.* Prepared by the Federal Writers' Project of
       Nebraska. Lincoln: Woodruff Printing Co., 1937. 87 pp.
679   *A Military History of Nebraska.* Lincoln, NE: Federal Writers'
       Project, 1939. 109 pp.
680   *Nebraska: Collected Works of Federal Writers' Project.* Federal
       Writers' Project Staff. Irvine, CA: Reprint Services, 1991.
681   *Nebraska: A Guide to the Cornhusker State.* Compiled and
       written by the Federal Writers' Project of the Works Progress
       Administration for the State of Nebraska. Sponsored by the
       Nebraska State Historical Society. New York: Viking Press,
       1939. 424 pp.
682   *Old Bellevue.* Federal Writers' Project of Nebraska. Papillion,
       NE: Papillion Times, 1937. 32 pp.
683   *Printing Comes to Lincoln.* Federal Writers' Project of Nebraska.
       Lincoln: Woodruff Printing Co., 1940. 80 pp.

Nevada
684   *Calendar of Annual Events in Nevada.* Compiled and written by
       Federal Writers' Project. Illustrated by Federal Art Project.
       Reno, NV: A. Carlisle, 1939.
685   *Nevada: A Guide to the Silver State.* Compiled by workers of the
       Writers' Program of the Work Projects Administration in the
       State of Nevada. Sponsored by Dr. Jeanne Elizabeth Wier,
       Nevada State Historical Society, Inc. Portland, OR: Binfords
       and Mort, 1940. 315 pp.
       WPA Guide to 1930s Nevada. Vintage West Series. Reno, NV:
       University of Nevada Press, 1991. 408 pp. paper.

New Hampshire
686   *New Hampshire: Collected Works of Federal Writers' Project.*
       Federal Writers' Project Staff. Irvine, CA: Reprint Services,
       1991.
687   *New Hampshire: A Guide to the Granite State.* Written by work-
       ers of the Federal Writers' Project of the Works Progress
       Administration for the State of New Hampshire. Boston, MA:
       Houghton Mifflin Company, 1938. 559 pp.
688   *The New Hampshire W.P.A. Writers' Project.* The New Hamp-
       shire Book Fair, November, 1940. Manchester, NH: Writers'
       Program of New Hampshire, 1940. 2 pp.

New Jersey

689   *Bergen County Panorama*. Written by workers of the Writers'
       Program of the Work Projects Administration in the State of
       New Jersey. Sponsored by the Bergen County Board of
       Chosen Freeholders, Hackensack, NJ. Elizabeth, NJ: Colby
       and McGowan, 1941. 356 pp.

690   *Entertaining a Nation: The Career of Long Branch*. Writers'
       Program, New Jersey. Sponsored by the City of Long Branch.
       Long Branch, NJ: Jersey Printing Co., 1940. 211 pp.

691   *Fair Lawn's Fire Fighters*. Fair Lawn, NJ, 1938. 30 pp.

692   *Livingston: The Story of a Community*. Written and illustrated by
       workers of the WPA Writers' Program of the Work Projects
       Administration in the State of New Jersey. Sponsored by the
       Township of Livingston. Caldwell, NJ: Progress Publishing
       Company, 1939. 166 pp.

693   *Matawan, 1686-1936*. Federal Writers' Project of New Jersey.
       Matawan, NJ: The Matawan Journal, 1936. 95 pp.
           Newark, NJ: Newick Brothers, Inc., 1936. Lithographed.
           95 pp.

694   *Monroe Township, Middlesex County, New Jersey, 1838-1938*.
       Federal Writers' Project of New Jersey. New Brunswick, NJ,
       1938. 140 pp.

695   *New Jersey: Collected Works of Federal Writers' Project*. Fed-
       eral Writers' Project Staff. Irvine, CA: Reprint Services,
       1991.

696   *New Jersey: A Guide to Its Present and Past*. Compiled and
       written by the Federal Writers' Project of the Works Progress
       Administration for the State of New Jersey. Sponsored by the
       Public Library of Newark and the New Jersey Guild Associ-
       ates. New York: Viking Press, 1939. 735 pp.
           The WPA Guide to 1930s New Jersey. Federal Writers' Project
           of the Works Progress Administration for New Jersey.
           New Brunswick, NJ: Rutgers University Press, 1986.
           750 pp.
           The WPA Guide to 1930s New Jersey. Federal Writers' Project
           of the Works Progress Administration Staff. New Bruns-
           wick, NJ: Rutgers University Press, 1989. 735 pp. paper.

697   *New Jersey: A Profile in Pictures*. Federal Writers' Project of
       New Jersey. New York: M. Barrows and Company, 1939.
       59 pp.

698   *Old Princeton's Neighbors.* Prepared by the Federal Writers' Project of New Jersey. Princeton, NJ: The Graphic Arts Press, 1939. 108 pp.

699   *Princeton's Fire Fighters, 1788-1938.* Prepared by the Federal Writers' Project of New Jersey. Princeton, NJ: Herald Press, 1938. 62 pp.

700   *Stories of New Jersey: Its Significant Places, People and Activities.* Prepared by the Federal Writers' Project of New Jersey. New York, NY: M. Barrows and Company, 1938. 442 pp.

701   *The Story of Dunellen, 1887-1937.* Written and illustrated by workers of the Federal Writers' Project of the Works Progress Administration. Dunellen, NJ: Art Color Printing Co., 1937. 111 pp.

702   *The Story of Wyckoff.* Wyckoff, NJ: Wyckoff News, 1939. 47 pp.

New Mexico

703   *New Mexico: Collected Works of Federal Writers' Project.* Federal Writers' Project Staff. Irvine, CA: Reprint Services, 1991.

704   *New Mexico: A Guide to the Colorful State.* Compiled by workers of the Writers' Program of the Work Projects Administration in the State of New Mexico. Sponsored by the Coronado Cuarto Centennial Commission and the University of New Mexico. New York: Hastings House, 1940. 458 pp.

       2nd edition. Albuquerque, NM: University of New Mexico Press, 1945.

       Revised edition, by Joseph Miller. Edited by Henry G. Alsberg. New York: Hastings House, 1953. 472 pp.

       Reprint of the 1940 edition. *The WPA Guide to Nineteen Thirties New Mexico.* Introduction by Marc Simmons. Tucson, AZ: University of Arizona Press, 1989. 530 pp. paper.

New York City

705   *Almanac for New Yorkers: 1937.* New York: Simon and Schuster, 1937. 128 pp.

706   *Almanac for New Yorkers: 1938.* New York: Modern Age, 1937. 118 pp.

707   *New York: Collected Works of Federal Writers' Project.* Federal Writers' Project Staff. 2 volumes. Irvine, CA: Reprint Services, 1991.

708   *New York City Guide: A Comprehensive Guide to the Five Boroughs of the Metropolis—Manhattan, Brooklyn, the Bronx, Queens, and Richmond.* Prepared by the Federal Writers' Project of the Works Progress Administration in New York City. Sponsored by the Guilds' Committee for Federal Writers' Publications, Inc. New York: Random House, 1939. 708 pp.

       The WPA Guide to New York City: The Federal Writers' Project Guide to 1930s New York. Prepared by the Federal Writers' Project of the Works Progress Administration in New York City. Introduction by William H. Whyte. New York: Pantheon, 1982. 680 pp.

709   *The New York City WPA Writers' Project: "This Work Pays Your Community."* New York, NY: The Project, 1939.

710   *New York Panorama: A Comprehensive View of the Metropolis.* Presented in a series of articles prepared by the Federal Writers' Project of the Works Progress Administration in New York City. New York: Random House, 1938. 526 pp. New York: Pantheon Books, 1984. 526 pp.

711   *WPA in New York City: The Record for 1938.* New York: WPA, 1939. 75 pp.

New York State

712   *Dutchess County.* Compiled by the workers of the Dutchess County Unit of the Federal Writers' Project of the Works Progress Administration in the State of New York. Sponsored by the Women's City and County Club of Dutchess County, New York. Philadelphia, PA: William Penn Association of Philadelphia, 1937. 166 pp.

713   *New York: A Guide to the Empire State.* Compiled by workers of the Writers' Program of the Work Projects Administration in the State of New York. Sponsored by New York State Historical Association. New York: Oxford University Press, 1940. 782 pp.

714   *Private Burial Grounds in Schenectady County, N. Y.* Federal Writers' Project of New York State. Albany, NY, 1938. 43 pp.

715   *Rochester and Monroe County.* Federal Writers' Project of the Works Progress Administration for the State of New York. Rochester, NY: Scrantom's, 1937. 460 pp.

716   *The Story of Five Towns: Inwood, Lawrence, Cedarhurst, Woodmere, and Hewlett, Nassau County, Long Island.* Compiled

by workers of the Writers' Program of the Work Projects Administration in the State of New York. Co-sponsored by Lawrence-Cedarhurst Chamber of Commerce. Rockville Centre, NY: Nassau Daily Review-Star, 1941. 70 pp.

717   *Sweetman and West Charlton Cemeteries, Saratoga County, New York.* Federal Writers' Project of New York State. Albany, NY, 1938. 75 pp.

718   *WPA in the Empire State.* Compiled and issued under the direction of Lester W. Herzog, New York State administrator of the Works Progress Administration. Albany, NY:Works Progress Administration, 1938. 30 pp.

North Carolina

719   *Charlotte: A Guide to the Queen City of North Carolina.* Compiled and written by the Writers' Project of the Work Projects Administration for the State of North Carolina. Sponsored by Hornet's Nest Post, No. 9, American Legion. Charlotte, NC: News Print House, 1939. 74 pp.

720   *North Carolina: Collected Works of Federal Writers' Project.* Federal Writers' Project Staff. Irvine, CA: Reprint Services, 1991.

721   *North Carolina: A Guide to the Old North State.* Compiled and written by the Federal Writers' Project of the Work Projects Administration for the State of North Carolina. Sponsored by North Carolina Department of Conservation and Development. Chapel Hill, NC: The University of North Carolina Press, 1939. 601 pp.

Reprint of 1939 edition. *North Carolina: The WPA Guide to the Old North State.* Federal Works Agency, Work Projects Administration, Federal Writers' Project Staff. Sponsored by North Carolina Department of Conservation and Development. New introduction by William S. Powell, editor. Columbia, SC: University of South Carolina Press, 1988. 600 pp.

722   *The North Carolina Guide*, edited by Blackwell Robinson. Federal Writers' Project of North Carolina. Revised edition. Chapel Hill, NC: University of North Carolina Press, 1955. 649 pp.

723   *North Carolina WPA: Its Story.* Raleigh: North Carolina Work Projects Administration, 1940. 47 pp.

724   *Raleigh: Capital of North Carolina.* By the Writers' Program of the Work Projects Administration in the State of North Caro-

lina. Sponsored by the Raleigh Sesquicentennial Commission. New Bern, NC: Owen G. Dunn Co., 1942. 170 pp.

North Dakota

725   *Bismarck, North Dakota: A Short History and a Guide to Points of Interest In and About the City.* Federal Writers' Project of North Dakota. Bismarck, ND, 1938. 20 pp.

726   *North Dakota: A Guide to the Northern Prairie State.* Written by workers of the Federal Writers' Project of the Works Progress Administration for the State of North Dakota. Sponsored by the State Historical Society of North Dakota. Fargo, ND: Knight Printing Company, 1938. 371 pp.

    2nd edition. New York: Oxford University Press, 1968. 352 pp.

    The WPA Guide to 1930s North Dakota. Bismarck, ND: State Historical Society of North Dakota, 1990. 376 pp.

Ohio

727   *Bryan and Williams County.* Compiled by workers of the Writers' Program of the Work Projects Administration in the State of Ohio. Sponsored by the City of Bryan. Gallipolis, OH: Downtain Printing Co., Inc., 1941. 117 pp.

728   *Chillicothe and Ross County.* Compiled and written by Federal Writers' Project of Ohio, Works Progress Administration. Columbus, OH: F. J. Heer Printing Co., 1938. 91 pp.

729   *Cincinnati: Glimpses of Its Youth.* Prepared by the Federal Writers' Project of Ohio. Cincinnati, OH, 1938. 42 pp.

730   *Cincinnati: A Guide to the Queen City and Its Neighbors.* Compiled by workers of the Writers' Program of the Work Projects Administration in the State of Ohio. Sponsored by the City of Cincinnati, Ohio. Cincinnati, OH: Wiesen-Hart Press, 1943. 570 pp.

    Cincinnati, 1788-1943 printed on the cover.

    Reprint. *The WPA Guide to Cincinnati.* Writers' Program of WPA, Ohio Staff. Introduction by Zane Miller. Preface by Harry Graff. Cincinnati, OH: Cincinnati History Society, 1987. 611 pp.

731   *Columbus Zoo Book: A Guide to the Columbus Zoo.* Compiled by workers of the Writers' Program of the Work Projects Administration in the State of Ohio. Sponsored by the Columbus Zoological Society. Columbus, OH, 1940. 59 pp.

A prefatory note states, "The manuscript was written by Thelma Walley and the art work was executed by Homer Seay."

732 *Fremont and Sandusky County.* Compiled by workers of the Writers' Program of the Work Projects Administration in the State of Ohio. Sponsored by the Ohio State Archaeological and Historical Society, Columbus. Co-sponsored by C. A. Hochenedel. Fremont, OH, 1940. Multilithed. 115 pp.

733 *A Guide to Lima and Allen County, Ohio.* Prepared by the Federal Writers' Project of the Works Progress Administration in Ohio. Lima, OH, 1938. 64 pp.

734 *Guide to Tuscarawas County.* Prepared by the Federal Writers' Project of the Works Progress Administration in Ohio. New Philadlephia, OH: Tucker Printing Co., 1939. 119 pp.

735 *Lake Erie, Vacationland in Ohio: A Guide to the Sandusky Bay Region.* Compiled by workers of Writers' Program of the Works Project Administration in the State of Ohio. Sponsored by the City of Sandusky in cooperation with Ohio's Lake Erie Vacationland, Inc. Sandusky, OH: Stephens Printing Co., 1941. 129 pp.

736 *Martins Ferry Sesquicentennial.* Prepared by the Federal Writers' Project of the Works Progress Administration in Ohio. Reproduced in cooperation with Martins Ferry Sesquicentennial Committee, Inc. Martins Ferry, OH, 1938. 10 pp.

737 *The National Road in Song and Story.* Federal Writer's Project of Ohio. Columbus, OH: Stoneman Press, 1940.

738 *Ohio: Collected Works of Federal Writers' Project.* Federal Writers' Project Staff. Irvine, CA: Reprint Services, 1991.

739 *The Ohio Guide.* Compiled by workers of the Writers' Program of the Work Projects Administration in the State of Ohio. Sponsored by the Ohio State Archaeological and Historical Society. New York: Oxford University Press, 1940. 634 pp.

740 *Springfield and Clark County, Ohio.* Compiled by workers of the Writers' Program of the Work Projects Administration in the State of Ohio. Sponsored by the Springfield Chamber of Commerce. Springfield, OH: Springfield Tribune Printing Company, 1941. 136 pp.

741 *They Built a City: 150 Years of Industrial Cincinnati.* Federal Writers' Project. Cincinnati, OH: Cincinnati Post, 1938. 402 pp.

742 *Urbana and Champaign County.* Compiled by workers of the Writers' Program of the Work Projects Administration in the

state of Ohio. Sponsored by the Urbana Lions Club. Urbana, OH: Gaumer Publishing Company, 1942. 147 pp.

743   *Warren and Trumbull County.* Compiled by the Federal Writers' Project of Ohio, Works Progess Administration. Sesquicentennial ed. Sponsored by Western Reserve Historical Celebration Committee. Warren, OH, 1938. 60 pp.

744   *WPA in Ohio.* Columbus, OH: Works Progress Administration, 1936. 1 folded sheet, with photos.

A booklet that describes "some achievements of Ohio's unemployed men and women who have been building a better Ohio and getting jobs and wages instead of the dole on useful WPA projects."

745   *Zanesville and Muskingum County.* Prepared by the Federal Writers' Project of the Works Progress Administration in Ohio. Reproduced in co-operation with Zanesville Chamber of Commerce. Zanesville, OH: Zanesville Chamber of Commerce, 1937. 38 pp.

Oklahoma

746   *Calendar of Events in Oklahoma.* Oklahoma City, OK: Tribune Publishing Co., 1938. 34 pp.

747   *Oklahoma: Collected Works of Federal Writers' Project.* Federal Writers' Project Staff. Irvine, CA: Reprint Services, 1991.

748   *Oklahoma: A Guide to the Sooner State.* Compiled by workers of the Writers' Program of the Work Projects Administration in the State of Oklahoma. Sponsored by the University of Oklahoma. Norman, OK: University of Oklahoma Press, 1941. 442 pp.

The WPA Guide to 1930s Oklahoma. Introduction by Anne Hodges Morgan. Restored essay by Angie Debo. Lawrence, KS: University Press of Kansas, 1986. 442 pp. paper.

Reprint of 1941 edition. *The WPA Guide to 1930s Oklahoma.* Lawrence, KS: University Press of Kansas, 1987. 568 pp.

749   *Tulsa: A Guide to the Oil Capital.* Compiled by workers of the Federal Writers' Project of the Works Progress Administration in the State of Oklahoma. Sponsored by the Tulsa Federation of Women's Clubs. Tulsa, OK: The Mid-West Printing Co., 1938. 79 pp.

Oregon

750   *Fire Prevention in Portland.* Federal Writers' Project. Portland,
       OR, 1938. 48 pp.
751   *History of Milwaukee, Oregon,* by Charles Oluf Olson. An un-
       finished manuscript prepared for the Federal Writers' Project.
       Milwaukee, OR: Milwaukee Historical Society, 1965.
752   *Mount Hood: A Guide.* New York: Duell, Sloan and Pearce, 1940.
       132 pp.
753   *Oregon: Collected Works of Federal Writers' Project.* Federal
       Writers' Project Staff. Irvine, CA: Reprint Services, 1991.
754   *Oregon: End of the Trail.* Compiled by workers of the Writers'
       Program of the Work Projects Administration in the State of
       Oregon. Sponsored by the Oregon State Board of Control.
       Portland, OR: Binfords and Mort, 1940. 549 pp.
       Revised edition, with added material by Howard McKinley
       Corning. Portland, OR: Binfords and Mort, 1951.
755   *Oregon WPA Writers' Project.* Portland, OR: The Project, 1940.
       2 pp.
756   *Portland Fire Alarm System.* Federal Writer's Project. Portland,
       OR, 1938. 30 pp.
757   *Portland Toy and Joymakers.* Compiled by workers of the Writ-
       ers' Program of the Work Projects Administration in the State
       of Oregon. Sponsored by Oregon Writers' Project and the
       Oregon State Board of Control. Portland, OR: The Project,
       1941. 23 pp.
       Cover title is *Portland Fire Department Toy and Joymakers.*
758   *Timberline Lodge: "A Year-Around Resort."* [Mount Hood Na-
       tional Forest.] Compiled by workers of the Writers' Program
       of the Work Projects Administration in the state of Oregon.
       Sponsored by Timberline Ski Club, 1940. 20 pp.
       A description of the completed structure, art work, and fur-
       nishings.

Pennsylvania

759   *Erie: A Guide to the City and County.* Philadelphia, PA: William
       Penn Association, 1938. 134 pp.
760   *The Floods of Johnstown.* Johnstown, PA: The Mayor's Commit-
       tee of the City of Johnstown, Pennsylvania, 1939. 36 pp.
761   *Hikes in Berks.* Compiled by the Berks County Unit, Federal
       Writers' Project of the Works Progress Administration for the
       Commonwealth of Pennsylvania. Sponsored by the Depart-

ment of Public Recreation, Reading, Pa. Philadelphia, PA: William Penn Association of Philadelphia, Inc., 1937. 47 pp.

762   *The Horse-Shoe Trail.* Written and compiled by the Philadelphia unit of the Federal Writers' Project of the Works Progress Administration for the Commonwealth of Pennsylvania. Sponsored by Henry N. Woolman, President, Horse-Shoe Trail Club, in Philadelphia, Pa. Philadelphia, PA: The William Penn Association of Philadelphia, Inc., 1938.

763   *Northampton County Guide.* Written and compiled by the Federal Writers' Project of the Work Projects Administration, Commonwealth of Pennsylvania. Sponsored by the Northampton County Historical and Genealogical Society. Bethlehem, PA: Times Publishing Co., 1939. 246 pp.

764   *Pennsylvania: Collected Works of Federal Writers' Project.* Federal Writers' Project Staff. Irvine, CA: Reprint Services, 1991.

765   *Pennsylvania: A Guide to the Keystone State.* Compiled by workers of the Writers' Program of the Work Projects Administration in the State of Pennsylvania. Co-sponsored by the Pennsylvania Historical Commission and the University of Pennsylvania. New York: Oxford University Press, 1940. 660 pp.

766   *Philadelphia: A Guide to the Nation's Birthplace.* Compiled by the Federal Writers' Project of Works Progress Administration, for the Commonwealth of Pennsylvania. Sponsored by the Pennsylvania Historical Commission. Philadelphia, PA: William Penn Association of Philadelphia, 1937. 704 pp.

   WPA Guide to Philadelphia. edited by E[dward] Digby Baltzell. Introduction by Richard J. Webster. Revised edition. Philadelphia, PA: University of Pennsylvania Press, 1988. 750 pp. paper.

   The WPA Guide to Philadelphia. Federal Writers' Project. 2nd Reprint edition. Philadelphia, PA: University of Pennsylvania Press, 1988. 704 pp.

767   *Pennsylvania Cavalcade.* Compiled by the Writers' Program of the Work Projects Administration in the Commonwealth of Pennsylvania. Co-sponsored by the Pennsylvania Federation of Historical Societies. Philadelphia, PA: University of Pennsylvania Press, 1942. 462 pp.

768   *A Picture of Clinton County.* Williamsport, PA: Commissioners of Clinton County, 1942. 195 pp.

769   *A Picture of Lycoming County.* Written and compiled by the Lycoming County Unit of the Pennsylvania Writers' Project of the Works Projects Administration. Sponsored by the Superintendent of Schools of Lycoming County, Frank H. Painter. Williamsport, PA: Commissioners of Lycoming County, 1939. 223 pp.

770   *Places to Play.* Compiled by the Workers of the Allegheny County Unit, Federal Writers' Project of the Works Progress Administration for the Commonwealth of Pennsylvania. Philadelphia, PA: William Penn Association, 1937. 40 pp.

       Cover title is *Places to Play in Allegheny County, North and South Parks.*

771   *Reading's Volunteer Fire Department: Its History and Traditions.* Federal Writers' Project of Berks County, Pennsylvania. Philadelphia, PA: William Penn Association, 1938. 263 pp.

Puerto Rico

772   *Puerto Rico: A Guide to the Island of Boriquén.* Compiled and written by the Puerto Rico Reconstruction Administration in co-operation with the Writers' Program of the Work Projects Administration. Sponsored by the Puerto Rico Department of Education. New York: The University Society, Inc., 1940. 409 pp.

Rhode Island

773   *Rhode Island: A Guide to the Smallest State.* Written by workers of the Federal Writers' Project of the Works Progress Administration for the State of Rhode Island. Boston, MA: Houghton Mifflin Company, 1937. 500 pp.

South Carolina

774   *Beaufort and the Sea Islands.* Prepared by Federal Writer's Project of the Works Progress Administration, South Carolina, 1938. Sponsored and published by the Clover Club. Savannah, GA: Review Printing Co., 1938. 47 pp.

775   *A History of Spartanburg County.* Compiled by the Spartanburg Unit of the Writers' Program of the Work Projects Administration in the State of South Carolina. Sponsored by the Spartanburg branch, American Association of University Women, South Carolina. Spartanburg, SC: Band and White, 1940. 304 pp.

776   *Publications, South Carolina Writers' Project,* WPA. SC, 1940.
       8 pp.
777   *South Carolina: Collected Works of Federal Writers' Project.* By
       the Federal Writers' Project Staff. Irvine, CA: Reprint Serv-
       ices, 1991.
778   *South Carolina: A Guide to the Palmetto State.* Compiled by
       workers of the Writers' Program of the Work Projects Ad-
       ministration in the State of South Carolina. Sponsored by
       Burnet R. Maybank, Governor of South Carolina. New York:
       Oxford University Press, 1941. 514 pp.
           South Carolina: The WPA Guide to the Palmetto State. Fed-
           eral Works Agency, Work Projects Administration, Fed-
           eral Writers' Project Staff. Introduction by Walter B.
           Edgar. Reprint of 1941 edition. Columbia, SC: University
           of South Carolina Press, 1988. 514 pp.
779   *The Story of the WPA in South Carolina.* Columbia, SC: The
       Information Service, South Carolina Works Progress Ad-
       ministration, 1936. 14 pp.

South Dakota
780   *Douglas County Tales and Towns.* Federal Writers' Project of
       South Dakota. Armour, SD: Armour Herald Printing, 1938.
       22 pp.
781   *Guide to Pierre: The Capital City and Its Vicinity.* Pierre, SD:
       State Publishing Co., 1937. 20 pp.
782   *Hamlin Garland Memorial.* Federal Writers' Project of South
       Dakota. Mitchell, SD: South Dakota Writers' League, 1939.
       33 pp.
783   *Mitchell, South Dakota: An Industrial and Recreational Guide.*
       Mitchell, SD, 1938. 32 pp.
784   *Pioneer Mitchell.* Pierre, SD: Hipple Printing Company, 1938.
       12 pp.
785   *Prairie Tamers of Miner County.* Prepared by the Federal Writ-
       ers' Project of the Works Progress Administration in South
       Dakota. Cooperating sponsor, Carthage Public Library
       Board. Mitchell, SD: Composed and printed in hand-set type
       by South Dakota Writers' League, 1939. 35 pp.
786   *South Dakota: Collected Works of Federal Writers' Project.*
       Federal Writers' Project Staff. Irvine, CA: Reprint Services,
       1991.
787   *A South Dakota Guide.* Compiled by the Federal Writers' Project
       of the Works Progress Administration for the State of South

Dakota. Sponsored by the State of South Dakota. Pierre, SD: State Publishing Company, 1938. 441 pp.

South Dakota: A Guide to the State. 2d ed. Completely revised by M. Lisle Reese. Sponsored by the State of South Dakota. New York: Hastings House, 1952. 421 pp.

Referred to as a "sequel to ... the South Dakota guide which was published in 1938."

788 *A Vacation Guide to Custer State Park in the Black Hills of South Dakota.* Pierre, SD: State Publishing Co., 1938. 32 pp.

Tennessee

789 *Tennessee: A Guide to the State.* Compiled and written by the Federal writers' Project of the Works Projects Administration for the State of Tennessee. Sponsored by Department of Conservation, Division of Information. New York: Viking Press, 1939. 558 pp.

The WPA Guide to Tennessee. Federal Writers' Project of the Work Projects Administration Staff. Reprint of 1939 edition. Foreword by Wilma Dykeman. Introduction by Jerrold Hirsch. Knoxville, TN: University of Tennessee Press, 1986. 608 pp.

Texas

790 *Beaumont: A Guide to the City and Its Environs.* Compiled and written by the Federal Writers' Project of the Work Projects Administration of the State of Texas. Sponsored by Beaumont Post 1806, Veterans of Foreign Wars of the U.S. Houston, TX: Anson Jones Press, 1939. 167 pp.

791 *The Denison Guide.* Federal Writers' Project of Texas. Denison, TX: Denison Chamber of Commerce, 1939. 29 pp.

792 *Houston: A History and Guide.* Sponsored by the Harris County Historical Society, Inc. Houston, TX: Anson Jones Press, 1942. 363 pp.

793 *Old Villita.* San Antonio, TX: The City of San Antonio, 1939. 22 pp.

794 *Port Arthur.* Sponsored by Hamilton Smith Post No. 797, Inc., Veterans of Foreign Wars of the U.S., Port Arthur. Houston, TX: Anson Jones Press, 1940. 164 pp.

795 *Randolph Field: A History and Guide.* Sponsored by the Commanding Officer, Randolph Field. New York: Devin-Adair, 1942. 156 pp.

796   *St. David's Through the Years.* Sponsored and published by the
      Betty Gilmer Chapter of St. David's Guild, St. David's Epis-
      copal Church. Austin, TX: St. David's Guild, St. David's
      Episcopal Church, 1942. 94 pp.

797   *San Antonio: An Authoritative Guide to the City and Its Environs.*
      San Antonio, TX: Clegg Co., 1938. 106 pp.
           Revised edition. *San Antonio: A History and Guide.* Spon-
           sored by the San Antonio Conservation Society. San An-
           tonio, TX: Clegg Company, 1941. 111 pp.

798   *Texas: Collected Works of Federal Writers' Project.* Federal
      Writers' Project Staff. Irvine, CA: Reprint Services, 1991.

799   *Texas: A Guide to the Lone Star State.* Compiled by workers of
      the Writers' Program of the Work Projects Administration in
      the State of Texas. Sponsored by the Texas State Highway
      Commission. New York: Hastings House, 1940. 718 pp.
           The WPA Guide to Texas. Edited by and Introduction by Don
           Graham. Texas Classics Series. Reprint of 1940 edition.
           Gulf Publications, 1986. 718 pp.
           The WPA Guide to Texas. Federal Writers' Project. Edited by
           Robert A. Calvert, and Anne Hodges Morgan. Reprint
           edition. Originally published in 1940. Austin, TX: Texas
           Monthly Press, 1986. 718 pp.

Utah

800   *Utah: Collected Works of Federal Writers' Project.* Federal
      Writers' Project Staff. Irvine, CA: Reprint Services, 1991.

801   *Utah: A Guide to the State.* Compiled by workers of the Writers'
      Program of the Work Projects Administration for the State of
      Utah. Sponsored by the Utah State Institute of Fine Arts.
      Co-sponsored by the Salt Lake County Commission. New
      York: Hastings House, 1941. 595 pp.

802   *Utah's Story.* Federal Writers' Project. Salt Lake City, UT, 1942.
      90 pp.

Vermont

803   *Vermont: Collected Works of Federal Writers' Project.* Federal
      Writers' Project Staff. Irvine, CA: Reprint Services, 1991.

804   *Vermont: A Guide to the Green Mountain State.* Written by
      workers of the Federal Writers' Project of the Works Progress
      Administration for the State of Vermont. Sponsored by the
      Vermont State Planning Board. Boston, MA: Houghton Mif-
      flin, 1937. 392 pp.

2nd edition, revised and enlarged. Edited by Ray Bearse.
Boston, MA: Houghton Mifflin, 1966. 456 pp.

3rd edition, revised. Edited by Ray Bearse. Boston, MA:
Houghton Mifflin, 1968. 452 pp.

805   *Vermont: A Profile of the Green Mountain State.* New York:
Fleming, 1941. 57 pp.

Virginia

806   *Dinwiddie County: "The Countrey of the Apamatica."* Richmond, VA: Whittet and Shepperson Printers, 1942. 302 pp.

807   *Sussex County: A Tale of Three Centuries.* Compiled by workers
of the Writers' Program of the Work Projects Administration
in the State of Virginia. Sponsored by the Sussex County
School Board. Richmond, VA: Whittet & Shepperson, 1942.
324 pp.

808   *Virginia: Collected Works of Federal Writers' Project.* Federal
Writers' Project Staff. Irvine, CA: Reprint Services, 1991.

809   *Virginia: A Guide to the Old Dominion.* Writers' Program of
Virginia. Compiled by workers of the Writers' Program of the
Work Projects Administration in the State of Virginia. Spon-
sored by James H. Price, Governor of Virginia. New York:
Oxford University Press, 1940. 699 pp.

Washington

810   *Washington: A Guide to the Evergreen State.* Compiled by workers of the Writers' Program of the Work Projects Administration in the State of Washington. Portland, OR: Binfords and
Mort, 1941. 687 pp.

Washington, District of Columbia

811   *Our Washington: A Comprehensive Album of the Nation's Capital in Words and Pictures.* Prepared by the Federal Writers'
Project of the Works Progress Administration. Sponsored by
the Guilds' Committee for Federal Writers' Publications, Inc.
Chicago, IL: A. C. McClurg and Co., 1939. 178 pp.

812   *Washington: City and Capital.* Federal Writers' Project of the
Works Progress Administration. Washington, DC: U.S. Government Printing Office, 1937. 1140 pp.

813   *Washington, D.C.: A Guide to the Nation's Capital.* Compiled by
workers of the Writers' Program of the Work Projects Administration for the District of Columbia. Sponsored by the

George Washington University. New York: Hastings House, 1942. 528 pp.

Washington, D.C.: A Guide to the Nation's Capital. Writers' Program of the District of Columbia. Edited by Randall [sic] Bond Truett. New York: Hastings House, 1968. Originally published in 1942.

A revised and condensed version of *Washington: City and Capital.*

The WPA Guide to Washington, D. C. Federal Writers' Project Staff. New York: Pantheon, 1983.

West Virginia

814   *Historic Romney, 1762-1937.* Federal Writers' Project of West Virginia. Romney, WV, 1937. 67 pp.

815   *West Virginia: Collected Works of Federal Writers' Project.* Federal Writers' Project Staff. Irvine, CA: Reprint Services, 1991.

816   *West Virginia: A Guide to the Mountain State.* Writers' Program of West Virginia. Compiled by workers of the Writers' Program of the Work Projects Administration in the State of West Virginia. Sponsored by the Conservation Commission of West Virginia. New York: Oxford University Press, 1941. 559 pp.

Wisconsin

817   *Portage.* Compiled and written by Federal Writers' Project of Wisconsin, Works Progress Administration. Sponsored by Portage Chamber of Commerce. Portage, WI: Portage Chamber of Commerce, 1938. 85 pp.

818   *Shorewood.* Federal Writers' Project of Wisconsin. Shorewood, WI: Village Board of Shorewood, 1939. 109 pp.

819   *The Story of Mineral Point, 1827-1941 Index.* Mineral Point, WI: Mineral Point Public Library, 1985. 15 pp.

820   *Wisconsin: Collected Works of Federal Writers' Project.* Federal Writers' Project Staff. Irvine, CA: Reprint Services, 1991.

821   *Wisconsin: A Guide to the Badger State.* Compiled by workers of the Writers' Program of the Work Projects Administration in the State of Wisconsin. Sponsored by the Wisconsin Library Association. New York: Duell, Sloan and Pearce, 1941. 651 pp.

Wyoming

822   *Wyoming: A Guide to Its History, Highways, and People*. Compiled by workers of the Writers' Program of the Work Projects Administration in the State of Wyoming. Sponsored by Dr. Lester C. Hunt, Secretary of State. New York: Oxford University Press, 1941. 490 pp.

Regional Guides

823   *Here's New England! A Guide to Vacationland*. Written and compiled by members of the Federal Writers' Project of the Works Progress Administration in the New England States. Sponsored by the New England Council, Boston. Boston, MA: Houghton Mifflin, 1939. 122 pp.

824   *The Intracoastal Waterway: Norfolk to Key West*. Compiled by Federal Writers' Project of the Works Progress Administration. Washington, DC: U. S. Government Printing Office, 1937. 143 pp.

825   *New England Hurricane: A Factual, Pictorial Record*. Written and compiled by members of the Federal Writers' Project of the Works Progress Administration in the New England states. Boston, MA: Hale, Cushman and Flint, 1938. 220 pp.

826   *The Ocean Highway: New Brunswick, New Jersey to Jacksonville, Florida*. Compiled and written by the Federal Writers' Project of the Works Progress Administration. New York: Modern Age Books, Inc., 1938. 244 pp.

827   *The Oregon Trail: The Missouri River to the Pacific Ocean*. Federal Writers' Project. Sponsored by Oregon Trail Memorial Association, Inc. New York: Hastings House, 1939. 244 pp.
Reprint. New York: Reprint House International, 1979.

828   *U.S. One, Maine to Florida*. Compiled and written by the Federal Writers' Project of the Works Progress Administration. Sponsored by the U.S. No. 1 Highway Association. New York: Modern Age Books, Inc., 1938. 344 pp.

Other Publications

829   *The Albanian Struggle in the Old World and New.* Federal
       Writer's Project of Massachusetts. Boston, MA: Writer, Inc.
       1939. 168 pp.

830   Alsberg, Henry G. *The American Guide Manual.* Washington,
       DC: Works Progress Administration, 1935. 86 pp.

       Reproduced from typewritten copy.

831   *American Guide Series.* Federal Writers' Project. Supplement of
       American Guide Series, Federal Writers' Project Catalog,
       Fall 1938. Washington, DC: U.S. Government Printing Of-
       fice, 1939.

832   *The American Guide Series: State Territorial Guides Prepared
       by WPA Writers' Program.* Reproduced from typewritten
       copy. Washington, DC: Library of Congress, General Refer-
       ence and Bibliography Division, 1944. 5 pp.

833   *American Stuff: An Anthology of Prose and Verse by Members of
       the Federal Writers' Project.* Federal Writers' Project. With
       16 prints by the Federal Art Project. New York: Viking Press,
       1937. 301 pp.

834   *American Stuff* [special issue of *Direction*, Vol. 1, No. 3, 1938].
       Federal Writers' Project. With eight prints by Federal Art
       Project.

835   *The Apache.* Prepared by Federal Writers' Project in Arizona.
       [*Arizona State Teachers College Bulletin* 20, No. 1, August,
       1939.] Flagstaff, AZ: Arizona State Teachers College, 1939.
       16 pp.

836   *The Armenians in Massachusetts.* Boston, MA: Armenian His-
       torical Society, 1937. 148 pp.

837   *The Assiniboines: From the Accounts of the Old Ones Told to
       First Boy (James Larpenter Long),* by the Writers' Program
       in Montana. Edited by and introduction by Michael Stephen
       Kennedy. Drawings by William Standing. The Civilization of
       the American Indian Series. Norman, OK: University of
       Oklahoma Press, 1961. 209 pp.

838   *Baseball In Old Chicago.* Chicago, IL: A. C. McClurg & Co.,
       1939. 64 pp.

839   *A Bid for Liberty: Being an Account of the Resolutions and
       Declarations of Independence Adopted in the Colony ....*
       Federal Writers' Project of the Works Progress Administra-

tion for the Commonwealth of Pennsylvania. Philadelphia,
PA: William Penn Association, 1937. 48 pp.

840   *Birds of the World: An Illustrated Natural History.* Chicago, IL:
A. Whitman and Co., 1938. 205 pp.

841   *Brief Containing Detailed Answers to Charges Concerning the
Federal Writers' Project Made by Witnesses Who Appeared
Before the Special Committee to Investigate Un-American
Activities, House of Representatives* [Washington, DC,
1938]. 43 pp.

842   *Bundle of Troubles, and Other Tarheel Tales,* edited by W. C.
Hendricks. Durham, NC: Duke University Press, 1943. 206
pp.

843   *Cape Cod Pilot,* by Jeremiah Digges [Josef Berger], with editorial
and research assistance of the members of the Federal Writ-
ers'project, Works Progress Administration for the State of
Massachusetts. Sponsored by Poor Richard Associates.
Provincetown, MA: Modern Pilgrim Press, 1937. 403 pp.
Foreword by Edward Gorey. New York: Viking, 1937.
Cambridge: MIT Press, 1969. 401 pp.
Boston, MA: Northeastern University Press, 1985. 401 pp.

844   *Catalog: American Guide Series.* Federal Writers' Project.
Washington, DC: U. S. Government Printing Office, 1938.
31 pp.

845   *Catalogue: WPA Writers' Program Publications: American
Guide Series.* American Life Series. Washington, DC: U.S.
Government Printing Office, 1941.
2nd ed. Evanston, IL: Chicago Historical Bookworks, 1990.
54 pp

846   *The Catamount,* 1937.
A mimeographed magazine issued by the Vermont Writers'
Project. Contains "five short stories, four of which were listed
as 'Distinctive Short Stories in American Magazines' in
Edward J. O'Brien's *Best Short Stories of 1938*" [Mangione,
The Dream and the Deal, p. 248].

847   *Cavalcade of the American Negro.* Chicago, IL: Diamond Jubilee
Exposition Authority, 1940. 95 pp.

848   *The Coast* (Spring 1937).
The only issue of an unofficial publication of writers on the
San Francisco Project.

849   *Conservation Education.* Federal Writers' Project. Philadelphia,
PA: Dunlap Printing Company, 1939.

850   *Drums and Shadows: Survival Studies Among the Georgia Coastal Negroes*, by the Savannah Unit, Georgia Writers' Project of the Work Projects Administration. Foreword by Guy B. Johnson. Photographs by Muriel and Malcolm Bell, Jr. Athens, GA: University of Georgia Press, 1940. 274 pp.

851   *The Fighting Finches*, by Dorothy Moulding Brown. Madison, WI: Federal Writers' Project, Folklore Section, 1937. 26 pp.

852   *The Film Index: A Bibliography.* Vol. I: *The Film as Art.* New York: Wilson, 1941. 780 pp.

       Reprint edition: New York: Arno, 1969.

853   *Final Report on Disposition of Unpublished Materials of WPA Writers' Program*, 8 April 1943, by Merle Colby. Washington, DC, 1943. 12 pp.

854   *Final Report on the WPA Program, 1935-43.* U.S. Federal Works Agency Staff. Washington, DC: Superintendent of Documents, U.S. Government Printing Office, 1943. 145 pp.

       Reprint edition. U. S. Government Documents Program Series. Westport, CT: Greenwood Press, 1976. 145 pp.

855   *Florida Seafood Cookery.* Prepared by the Federal Writers' Project in Florida. Tallahassee,FL: Department of Agriculture, 1956. 88 pp.

856   *Frontier and Midland* (Winter 1938).

       Edited by Harold G. Merriam. Focused on writers from west of the Mississippi. Contained 44 stories and poems by Federal Writers' Project writers.

857   *Gli Italiani di New York.* [Italian] New York: Labor Press, 1939. 242 pp.

       Reprint edition. *The Italians of New York.* The American Immigration Collection. New York: Arno, 1969. 241 pp.

858   *God Bless the Devil: Liars' Bench Tales.* Chapel Hill, NC: University of North Carolina Press, 1940. 254 pp.

859   *Gumbo Ya-Ya: A Collection of Louisiana Folk Tales.* Writers' Program of Louisiana. Compiled by Lyle Saxon, State Director, Edward Dreyer, Assistant State Director, and Robert Tallant, special writer. Boston, MA: Houghton Mifflin, 1945. 581 pp.

       Reprint edition, New York: Johnson Reprint, 1969. Drawings by Caroline Durieux. Jacket and decorations by Roland Duvernet. Illustrated with photos. 581 pp.

860   *Hands That Built New Hampshire: The Story of Granite State Craftsmen Past and Present.* Writers' Project of New Hampshire. Brattleboro, VT: Stephen Daye Press, 1940. 288 pp.

861 *The Harmony Society in Pennsylvania.* Federal Writers' Project. Philadelphia, PA: William Penn Association, 1937. 38 pp.

862 *The Havasupai and the Hualapai.* Federal Writers' Project. [*Arizona State Teachers College Bulletin* 21, No. 5.] Flagstaff, AZ: State Teachers College, 1940. 35 pp.

863 *Historical and Pictorial Review: National Guard of the State of Wyoming, 1940.* Baton Rouge, LA: Army and Navy Publishing Company, 1940.

864 *Hoosier Tall Stories.* Federal Writers' Project. Indianpolis, IN, 1939.

865 *The Hopi.* Preparedby Federal Writers' Project. Flagstaff, AZ: State Teachers College, 1937. 26 pp.

866 *Immigrant America: A Narrative Given On New Citizen's Day, June 1, 1939.* Prepared by workers for the Federal Writers' Project in Utah. Salt Lake City, UT, 1939. 28 pp.

867 *Immigrant Settlements in Connecticut: Their Growth and Characteristics,* by Samuel Koenig. Works Progress Administration, Federal Writers' Project for the State of Connecticut. Hartford, CT: Connecticut State Department of Education, 1938. 67 pp.

868 *The Italian Theatre in San Francisco: Being a History of the Italian-Language Operatic, Dramatic, and Comedic Productions Presented in the San Francisco Bay Area Through the Depression Era, With Reminiscences of the Leading Players and Impresarios of the Times.* 120 pp. San Bernardino, CA: Borgo Press, 1991.

   Provides history of contributions of Italian culture to theater as it developed in San Francisco, based on a monograph originally compiled as a mimeographed volume by The Federal Writers' Project of the Works Progress Administration. Includes two parts, "The Popular Theatre" and "The Italian Theatre." This new edition has been reset and includes an index of productions, persons, and companies.

869 *The Italians of New York.* A survey prepared by workers of the Federal Writers' Project of the Works Progress Administration in New York City. New York: Random House, 1938. 241 pp.

870 *Jewish Families and Family Circles of New York.* [Yiddish] New York, 1939. 206 pp.

871 *Jewish Hometown Associations and Family Circles in New York: The WPA Yiddish Writers' Group Study.* Edited by Hannah Kliger. Introduction and Afterword by Hannah Kliger. The

Modern Jewish Experience Series. Bloomington, IN: Indiana University Press, 1992. 208 pp.

872   *The Jewish Landsmanschaften of New York.* [Yiddish] New York, NY: I. L. Peretz Yiddish Writers' Union, 1938. 397 pp.

873   *Jobs: the WPA Way.* Washington, DC: Government Printing Office, 1936. 48 pp.

874   *Labor History of Oklahoma.* Oklahoma City, OK: A. M. Van Horn, 1939. 120 pp.

875   *Lamps on the Prairie: A History of Nursing in Kansas.* Compiled by the Writers' Program of the Work Projects Administration in the State of Kansas. Emporia, KS: Emporia Gazette Press 1942. 292 pp.
      Reprint. Topeka: Ives, 1962.
      New York: Garland, 1984. The History of American Nursing Series. 292 pp.

876   *Lay My Burden Down: A Folk History of Slavery, edited by B. A. Botkin.* Federal Writers' Project. Chicago, IL: University of Chicago Press, 1945. 285 pp.

877   *Libraries and Lotteries: A History of the Louisville Free Public Library.* Compiled by workers in the Service Division of the Work Projects Administration in the State of Kentucky. Preface by William R. Breyer and Edward L. Kinkade. American Guide Series. Cynthiana, KY: The Hobson Press, 1944. 300 pp.

878   *Manual of the Survey of Historical Records.* Federal Writers' Project. Washington, DC, 1936.

879   *Map of California.* Federal Writers' Project of the Works Progress Administration. Washington, DC: The Project, 1939. 62 x 52 cm.
      Includes maps of Los Angeles with inset of Los Angeles and San Francisco. Also includes inset map of transportation routes.

880   *Material Gathered,* 1936.
      Included more than 100 single-spaced mimeographed pages of poems, short stories, and a verse play. Produced a literary magazine as an unofficial Federal Writers' Project publication to provide a sample of what the Project writers could do.

881   *Military History of Kentucky, Chronologically Arranged.* Written by workers of the Federal Writers' Project of the Works Progress Administration. Frankfort, KY: State Journal, 1939. 493 pp.

882 *The Navaho*. Material prepared by Federal Writers' Project of the
     W.P.A. [*Arizona State Teachers College Bulletin* 18, No. 4,
     November 1937.] Flagstaff, AZ: Arizona State Teachers College, 1938. 21 pp.
     2nd printing. Flagstaff, AZ: Arizona State Teachers College, 1938. 22 pp.

883 *Nebraska Folklore*. 2 Vols. Lincoln, NE: Woodruff Printing Company, 1939-40.

884 *The Negro in New York: An Informal Social History*. Edited by Roi Ottley and W. J. Weatherby. New York: New York Public Library and Oceana, 1967. 328 pp.

885 *The Negro in Virginia*. Compiled by Workers in the Writers' Program of the Work Projects Administration in the State of Virginia. New York: Hastings House Publishers, 1940. Reprinted, 1969.

886 *Negro Newcomers in Detroit*, by George Edmund Haynes. In *The Negro in Washington*, prepared by the Federal Writers' Project, pp. 68-90. Part of *Washington: City and Capital*. The American Negro, His History and Literature Series. New York: Arno Press, 1969.

887 *The Negroes of Nebraska*. Lincoln, NE: Woodruff Printing Co., 1940. 48 pp.

888 *New Masses* (10 May 1938).

889 *New Republic*. "Federal Poets: An Anthology." 11 May 1938.

890 *Origin of Nebraska Place Names*. Prepared by the Federal Writers' Project of Nebraska. Lincoln, NE, 1938. 28 pp.

891 *Origins of Utah Place Names*. Material prepared by the Federal Writers' Project of Utah. Salt Lake City, UT, 1938. 36 pp.

892 *Our Federal Government and How It Functions*. Compiled and written by the Federal Writers' Project [Washington, DC] of the Works Progress Administration. New York: Hastings House, 1939. 234 pp.

893 *Palmetto Pioneers: Six Stories of Early South Carolinians*. Compiled, written and illustrated by Federal Writers' Project of the Works Progress Administration. Sponsored by the Division of Adult Education, State Department of Education, South Carolina. Columbia, SC, 1938. 81 pp.

894 *The Papago*. Material prepared by Federal Writers' Project of Arizona. [*Arizona State Teachers College Bulletin* 20, No. 3, October 1939.] Flagstaff, AZ: Arizona State Teachers College, 1939. 16 pp.

895   *Pioneer Religion.* Robert E. Carlson, editor. Nebraska Folklore
       Pamphlets, No. 26. Nebraska Writers' Project in cooperation
       with the State Superintendent of Public Instruction. Lincoln,
       NE: WPA Writers' Program of the Work Projects Admini-
       stration in the State of Nebraska, 1940. 14 pp.

896   *Pioneer Tales of San Bernardino County.* WPA Federal Writers'
       Project. West Coast Studies, No. 2. Reprint of 1940 edition.
       San Bernardino, CA: Borgo Press, 1989. 60 pp.

897   *Poetry.* "Federal Poets Number." 52 (July 1938). With supple-
       mentary articles by Malcolm Cowley, Alfred Kreymborg.

       Federal Poets' Number which hopes to provide "more ade-
       quate recognition of the the poets" who are members of the
       Federal Writers' Project. Contributors to the volume include
       Kenneth Fearing, Willard Maas, Dorothy Van Ghent, Alfred
       Hayes, Raymond E. F. Larsson, William Pillin, Mark Turby-
       fill, James Daly, Helen Neville, Miriam Allen de Ford, Harold
       Rosenberg, S. Funaroff, Virgil Geddes, Harry Roskolenko,
       and Margaret Walker.

898   *Reptiles and Amphibians: An Illustrated Natural History.* Pre-
       pared by workers of the Federal Writers' Project of the Works
       Progress Administration in the city of New York. Decorations
       by WPA Federal Art Project in the City of New York. Spon-
       sored by the Guilds' Committee for Federal Writers' Publi-
       cations, Inc. Chicago, IL: A. Whitman and Co., 1939. 253 pp.

899   *A Report of Progress: Federal Project One in Ohio.* Prepared by
       the Federal Writers' Project of Ohio. Columbus, OH, 1936.
       49 pp.

900   *Selected Bibliography: Illinois, Chicago and Its Environs.* Fed-
       eral Writers' Project of the Works Progress Administration in
       Illinois. Photoprinted. Chicago, IL, 1937. 58 pp.

901   *Selective and Critical Bibliography of Horace Mann.* Compiled
       by workers of the Federal Writers' Project of the Works
       Progress Administration in the State of Massachusetts. Issued
       by Commissioner of Education, James G. Reardon in coop-
       eration with the Boston School Department. Roxbury, MA:
       Designed and printed by the Roxbury Memorial High School
       (Boys) Printing Department, 1937. 54 pp.

902   *Shucks,* 1936. Mimeographed.

       A 23-page compilation of poems, articles, and stories, pro-
       duced by the Nebraska Writers' Project for "recreation and
       practice."

903   *Skiing in the East: The Best Trails and How to Get There.*
       Prepared by the Federal Writers' Project of New York City.
       New York, NY: M. Borrows & Company, 1939. 334 pp.

904   *Slave Narratives: A Folk History of Slavery in the United States
       From Interviews with Former Slaves.* Federal Writers' Pro-
       ject. Sponsored by the Library of Congress. Illustrated with
       photographs. 17 vols. Vol. 1: "Alabama Narratives." Vol. 2:
       "Arkansas Narratives." Vol. 3: "Florida Narratives." Vol. 4:
       "Georgia Narratives." Vol. 5: "Indiana Narratives." Vol. 6:
       "Kansas Narratives." Vol. 7: "Kentucky Narratives." Vol. 8:
       "Maryland Narratives." Vol. 9: "Mississippi Narratives."
       Vol. 10: "Missouri Narratives." Vol. 11: "North Carolina
       Narratives." Vol. 12: "Ohio Narratives." Vol. 13: "Oklahoma
       Narratives." Vol. 14: "South Carolina Narratives." Vol. 15:
       "Tennessee Narratives." Vol. 16: "Texas Narratives." Vol.
       17: "Virginia Narratives." Washington, DC: Library of Con-
       gress, 1944.
       Reprint. St. Clair Shores, MI: Scholarly Press, 1976.
       Contains typescript versions of interviews collected by the
       Federal Writers' Project during 1936-1938, Work Projects
       Administration, for the District of Columbia. Assembled by
       the Library of Congress project.

905   *Sodbusters: Tales of Southeastern South Dakota.* Alexandria,
       SD: Printed by the South Dakota Writers' League at the
       Alexandria Herald, 1938. 27 pp.

906   *South Carolina Folk Tales: Stories of Animals and Supernatural
       Beings.* Columbia, SC: University of South Carolina Press,
       1941. 122 pp.

907   *The Southern Harmony Songbook,* by William Walker. Repro-
       duced, with an introduction by the Federal Writers' Project of
       Kentucky of the Works Progress Administration. Sponsored
       by the Young Men's Progress Club, Benton, Kentucky. New
       York: Hastings House, 1939. 336 pp.

908   *The Story of the Negro in Los Angeles County,* by Octavia B.
       Vivian. Compiled by Federal Writers' Project of the Works
       Progress Administration under the supervision of Hugh Har-
       lan, 1936. 43 pp.
       Photocopy. San Francisco, CA: R. and E. Research Associ-
       ates, 1970. 43 pp.

909   *Survey of Negroes in Little Rock and North Little Rock.* Writers'
       Program of Little Rock, Arkansas. Little Rock, AR: Urban
       League of Greater Little Rock, 1941. 101 pp.

910   *The Swedes and Finns in New Jersey.* Written and illustrated by
        the Federal Writers' Project of the Works Progress Admini-
        stration in the State of New Jersey. Introduction by Dr.
        Amandus Johnson. Sponsored by the New Jersey commission
        to commemorate the 300th anniversary of the settlement by
        the Swedes and Finns on the Delaware, D. Stewart Craven,
        Chairman. Bayonne, NJ: Jersey Printing Company, Inc.,
        1938. 165 pp.

911   *Terror Against the People: The Story of the WPA Witch Hunt.*
        New York: Joint Committee to Defend W.P.A. Workers,
        1937. 13 pp.

912   *Tales of Pioneer Pittsburgh.* Prepared by the Federal Writers'
        Project of Pittsburgh. Philadelphia, PA: William Penn Asso-
        ciation, 1937. 28 pp.

913   *These Are Our Lives, As Told By the People and Written by
        Members of the Federal Writers' Project of the Works Pro-
        gress Administration in North Carolina, Tennessee, and
        Georgia.* Federal Writers' Project. Preface by W. T. Couch.
        Chapel Hill, NC: University of North Carolina Press, 1939.
        421 pp.
        Reprint. *These Are Our Lives.* The American Negro, His
             History and Literature Series. New York, Arno Press,
             1969. 421 pp.
        Reprint. St. Clair Shores, MI: Somerset Publishers, 1972.
             421 pp.
        Reprint. New York: Norton, 1975. 421 pp.

914   *Topical Digest of the Wisconsin Statutes Relating to Public
        Welfare.* Madison, 1936. 143 pp.

915   *Tropical Fruits in Florida With Commercial Possibilities.* Talla-
        hassee, FL: Florida State Department of Agriculture, 1941.
        43 pp.

916   *Whaling Masters.* Federal Writers' Project. New Bedford, MA:
        Old Dartmouth Historical Society, 1938. 314 pp.

917   *The White House.* Federal Writers' Project. Extract from *Wash-
        ington: City and Capital.* Washington, DC: U.S. Government
        Printing Office, 1937. 30 pp.

918   *Who's Who in Aviation: A Directory of Living Men and Women
        Who Have Contributed to the Growth of Aviation in the
        United States.* Writers' Program of the Work Projects Ad-
        ministration in the State of Illinois. Chicago, IL: Ziff-Davis
        Publishing Co., 1942. 486 pp.

919   *Who's Who in the Zoo: Natural History of Mammals.* New York: Halcyon, 1937. 211 pp.
920   *Wisconsin Circus Lore.* Compiled by workers of the Writers' Program of the Work Projects Administration in the State of Wisconsin. Madison, WI, 1937. 58 pp.
921   *Wisconsin Indian Place Legends,* by Dorothy Moulding Brown. Madison, WI: Folklore Section, Federal Writers' Projects, 1936. 50 pp.
922   *Wisconsin Mushrooms.* Prepared by the Federal Writers' Project of Wisconsin. Madison, WI, 1937. 13 pp.
923   *WPA Writers' Program Publications Catalogue: The American Guide Series.* WPA Staff. The American Life Series. Washington, DC: Government Printing Office, 1941. 52 pp.
      WPA Writers' Program Publications. Evanston, IL: Chicago Historical Bookworks, 1990. 53 pp.
      2nd edition. Evanston, IL: Chicago Historical Bookworks, 1990. 54 pp. paper.

Archives

924   Henry G. Alsberg to State Directors of the Federal Writers' Project, 9 June 1937.
925   Henry G. Alsberg to State Directors of the Federal Writers' Project, 30 July 1937. [Suggestions for collecting ex-slave interviews.] Work Projects Administration Federal Writers' Project Materials. Archive of Folk Song, Library of Congress, Washington, DC.
926   *Archives of the Federal Writers' Project.* Series One: Printed and Mimeograph Publications in the Surviving FWP Files, 1933-1943, Excluding State Guides. Harvester Microfilm Collection. Woodbridge, CT: Research Publicatons, 1992.
927   George Cronyn to Edwin Bjorkman, State Director, Federal Writers' Project, North Carolina. Ex-Slave Narratives. Work Projects Administration Federal Writers' Project Materials. Archive of Folk Song, Library of Congress, Washington, DC.
928   Botkin, Benjamin A. "Manual for Folklore Studies." Federal Writers' Project Materials, Archive of Folk Song, Library of Congress, Washington, DC.
929   Bourne, Frances T. "Report and Recommendation for Disposition of Records of the Federal Writers' Project." Library of Congress, Washington, DC, 29 July 1949.
930   Brown, Sterling A. 20 June 1937. "Notes by an Editor on Dialect Usage in Accounts by Interviews with Ex-Slaves. (To Be

Used in Conjunction with Supplementary Instructions 9E.)" Work Projects Administration Federal Writers' Project Materials. Archive of Folk Song, Library of Congress, Washington, DC.

931   Federal Writers' Project, (unprocessed papers) Library of Congress Manuscripts Division.

932   Federal Writers' Project files, Archive of Folk Song, Library of Congress, Washington, DC.

933   Federal Writers' Project Files, Records of the Work Projects Administration, National Archives, Washington, DC.

934   The Federal Writers' Project Papers of the Regional Director, William Terry Couch, Southern Historical Collection, University of North Carolina at Chapel Hill.

935   Lomax, John A. 22 April 1937. "Supplementary Instructions #9-E to the American Guide Manual." Work Projects Administration Federal Writers' Project Materials. Archive of Folk Song, Library of Congress, Washington, DC.

936   U.S. Congress, House of Representatives, Special Committee on Un-American Activities. *Investigation of Un-American Propaganda Activities in the United States.* Hearing on H.R. 282, 75th Congress, 3rd Session, 1938.

937   U.S. Congress, House of Representatives, Subcommittee of the Committee on Appropriations. *Hearing on H.R. 130*, 76th Congress, 1st session, 1939-1940.

938   Mrs. Wharton to B. A. Botkin, 25 February 1941. Comments on the Slave Narratives. Work Projects Administration Federal Writers' Project Materials. Archive of Folk Song, Library of Congress, Washington, DC.

939   Work Projects Administration, Federal Writers' Project, National Archives, Washington, DC.

940   Work Projects Administration Federal Writers' Project Materials. Archive of Folk Song, Library of Congress, Washington, DC.

941   Work Projects Administration Records, Record Group 69, National Archives, Washington, DC. [Includes the Dies Committee files, Federal Writers' Project files, Division of Information files, Service Division files, and state files.]

942   "WPA Writers' Program Records, Appraisal Sheet." Work Projects Administration Federal Writers' Project Materials. Archive of Folk Song, Library of Congress, Washington, DC.

A List of Federal Writers' Project Writers

The writers are listed alphabetically followed by the state abbreviation for the particular Writers' Project. In some cases the city projects within a state are listed after the state affiliation. In a few cases the writers transferred to a different project. Individuals whose names are not listed with a state or city designation worked with the national offices.

A

Abel, Lionel—IL Chicago, NY City
Aiken, Conrad—MA
Algren, Nelson—IL Chicago
Aswell, James—TN

B

Balch, Jack S.—NY City, MO
Baldwin, Aubrey—PA
Beanne, Everett—NY City
Bellow, Saul—IL Chicago
Berger, Josef—MA
Billington, Ray—MA
Bodenheim, Maxwell—NY City
Bontemps, Arna—IL Chicago
Botkin, Benjamin A.
Breit, Harvey—CA
Brown, Sterling A.
Bukin, Arthur—NE

C

Carlson, Robert—NE

Cheever, John—NY City
Christensen, Fred—NE
Colby, Merle—MA
Conrad, Earl—NY City
Conroy, Jack—IL Chicago
Corey, Paul—NY State
Corning, Howard McKinley—OR
Cuney, Waring—NY City

D

Dahlberg, Edward—NY City
Daly, James
deFord, Miriam Allen—CA
De Sola, Ralph—NY City
Dewey, G. Gordon—NE
Dickson, Harrison—MO
Dorais, Leon—CA Los Angeles
Dunham, Katherine—IL Chicago

E

Edwards, Paul—NY City

Eiseley, Loren—NE
Ellison, Ralph—NY City
Engelhorn, Elmer—NY City
Estavan, Lawrence—CA

F

Fearing, Kenneth—NY City
FitzGerald, William C.—MA
Foreman, Carl—CA
Frederick, John T.—IL Chicago
French, Paul Comly—PA
Funaroff, Sol—NY City

G

Gable, J. Harris—NE
Geddes, Virgil
Gellert, Lawrence—NY City
Getty, Norris—NE
Gibson, William—NY City
Gleason, Margaret—CA
Gould, Joe—NY City
Gross, Bella—NY City

H

Harris, Reed
Hatcher, Harlan—OH
Hawks, Mary—MA
Hayes, Charles
Hays, H. R.
Herrmann, John—NY City
Hill, Abraham—NY City
Hoke, Travis—NY City
Hopper, James—CA

Howard, Robert West—NY State
Hurston, Zora Neale—FL

I

Ignatin, Irving—PA
Ignatow, David—NY City

J

Johns, Orrick—NY City

K

Kees, Weldon—NE
Kemp, Harry—NY City
Kerr, Florence—MO
Kinkead, Robin—CA

L

Larsson, Raymond E. F.—CA
Lengyel, Cornel—CA
LeSeur, Meridel—MN
Levitt, Saul—NY City
Lewis, Roscoe E.—VA
Lomax, John A.

M

Maas, Willard—NY City
Macleod, Norman—NY City
Manoff, Arnold—IL
McCann, Angelica—CA
McDaniel, Eluard Luchell—CA
McElroy, Walter—CA
McGraw, James—NY City
McHugh, Vincent—NY City
McKay, Claude—NY City
Mean, Frank—IL Chicago

Moon, Henry Lee—NY City
Moss, Carlton—NY City
Motley, Willard—IL Chicago

N

Netboy, Anthony—NY City
Neville, Helen—NY City
Nugent, Richard—NY City

O

Offord, Carl—NY City
Olsen, Tillie—CA

P

Partnow, Hyde—NY
Patchen, Kenneth—CA
Pergament, Lola
Pillin, William—IL
Poston, Ted—NY City
Putnam, Samuel—PA

R

Radenzel, Ed—CA
Rader, Guy H.—MT
Rahv, Philip—NY City
Randolph, Vance—MO
Rexroth, Kenneth—CA
Robinson, Harry—NY City
Rogers, J. A.—NY City
Roi, Ottley—NY City
Rollins, William, Jr.—NY City
Rosen, A. T.—NY City
Rosenberg, Harold—NY City
Rosenfeld, Isaac—IL
Roskolenko, Harry—NY City
Ross, Sam—IL Chicago

S

Sabsay, Nahum—CA
Sassaman, Grant—PA
Saxe, Arthur M.—MA
Saxon, Lyle—LA
Schlasinger, Ethel—ND
Shannon, Opal—IA
Shay, Frank—NY City
Sheehan, Elizabeth—NE
Siegel, Eli—NY City
Snelson, Floyd—NY City
Spector, Herman—NY
Spring, Agnes Wright—NE
Stahlberg, John—MT
Steinbeck, John—CA
Swenson, May—NY

T

Tarry, Ellen—NY City
Turbyfill, Mark

U

Ulrich, Mabel—MN
Umland, Rudolph—NE

V

Vaerlen, Basil—CA
Van Ghent, Dorothy—CA
Van Olinda, Walter K.—NY
  City
Vogel, Joseph—NY City

W

Walker, Margaret—IL Chicago
Weinrebe, Baruch A.—NY City

Widen, Ruth—NY City
Wilder, Charlotte—NY City
Wilhelmson, Carl—CA
Williams, Cal—WY
Williamson, Simon—NY City
Wirth, Nicholas—NY
Wright, Gwendolyn—CA
Wright, Richard—IL Chicago,
    NY City

Y

Yerby, Frank—IL Chicago
Yezierska, Anzia—NY City

Section 3

Recordings

943   Banks, Ann, ed. *First-Person America: Voices from the Thirties.* Washington, DC: National Public Radio, 1981. 3 cassettes, 1 7/8 ips. Guide, 12 pp.

944   *A Breath of the Carolina Low Country* [Gullah], by Dick Reeves. Charleston, SC: Lenwal Enterprises, 1963. 1 disc, 12 in., 33 1/3 rpm, mono. L 252.

945   Broonzy, Big Bill. *Good Time Tonight.* Roots n' Blues Series. New York, NY: Columbia Records, 1990. 1 compact disc, digital, mono. CK 46219.

       Includes "W.P.A. Rag" among songs recorded between 1930 and 1940.

946   Broonzy, Big Bill. *Good Time Tonight.* Program notes by Lawrence Cohn. Roots n' Blues Series. New York, NY: Columbia, 1990. 1 sound disc, 12 in., 33 1/3 rpm, mono. C 46219.

       Includes "WPA Rag." Contains unissued recordings.

947   Broonzy, Big Bill. *Unissued Test Pressings.* Le Hot Club de France Archive Series. [United States:] Milan: BMG distributor, 1992. 1 compact disc, digital. 7313835625-2.

       Includes "WPA Blues."

948   Emrich, Duncan, ed. *Animal Tales Told in the Gullah Dialect,* told by Albert H. Stoddard of Savannah, Georgia. Folklore of the United States Series. Washington, DC: Library of Congress, Division of Music Recording Laboratory, 1955. 3 discs, 12 in., 33 1/3 rpm, mono. AAFS L44-46.

949   *Evolution of the Blues Song.* Narration by Jon Hendricks. New York, NY: Columbia, 1961. 1 sound disc, 12 in., 33 1/3 rpm, stereo. CS 1583.

       Includes "W.P.A. Blues."

950   Hendricks, Jon. *Evolution of the Blues Song*. Program notes by
       Jon Hendricks. New York, NY: Columbia, 1961. 1 sound
       disc, 12 in., 33 1/3 rpm. CL 1583.
       Presents blues songs and spirituals with narration by Jon
       Hendricks "as presented at the Monterey Jazz Festival 1960."
       Includes "W.P.A. Blues." Performers include "Big" Miller,
       "Pony" Poindexter, Jimmy Witherspoon, the Ike Isaacs Trio,
       Ben Webster, and Hannah Dean.

951   *Louis Armstrong and His Orchestra, 1939-1940*. The Classics
       Chronological Series. [Europe:] Classics, 1991. 1 compact
       disc, digital. No. 615.
       Includes "W.P.A."

952   *News and the Blues: Telling It Like It Is*. Notes by Pete Welding.
       Roots n' Blues Series. New York, NY: Columbia, 1990. 1
       sound disc, 12 in., 33 1/3 rpm, stereo. C 46217.
       Includes "WPA Blues" perfomed by Casey Bill Weldon.
       Other performers include Bessie Smith, Blind Willie
       Johnson, Charlie Patton, Bill Gaither, and Big Bill Broonzy.

953   *Rhapsody in Concert*. Performance Tape Series. School of Music,
       Eastern New Mexico University, 1992. 1 sound cassette.
       Performance presented on 7 February 1992 included
       "W.P.A." Program Notes. Shelved in the Listening Center.

954   *Songs of the Depression: Happy Days Are Here Again*. Sung and
       played by various performers from original recordings. Camp
       Hill, PA: Book-of-the-Month Records, 1980. 2 discs, 12 in.,
       33 1/3 rpm, mono.
       Includes "Brother, Can You Spare a Dime?" "Underneath the
       Arches," and "W.P.A."

955   *Voices From the Past*. Alexandria, VA: Audio-Forum, Inc. 1
       cassette, 1 7/8 ips, 2-track, mono.

956   *Will Weldon (Casey Bill)*. Blues Documents Series. Vienna: RST
       Records, 1982. 1 disc, 12 in., 33 1/3 rpm, stereo. BD-605.
       Includes "W.P.A. Blues."

Index

References are to entry numbers. Works about the Federal Writers' Project are usually listed by main title.

158

The Federal Writers' Project

About the Author

JEUTONNE P. BREWER (B.A., Harding College; M.A., Ph.D., University of North Carolina at Chapel Hill) is an Associate Professor of English at the University of North Carolina at Greensboro, where she teaches courses in linguistics. She is a member of the Linguistic Society of America, Southeastern Conference on Linguistics, Association of Computers and Humanities, Oral History Association, and American Dialect Society. Her published essays about the language use in the ex-slave narratives collected by the Federal Writer's Project reflect her research interests in language variation and American dialects. Dr. Brewer is compiling a bibliography of the WPA; this book is an important component of that research project. She is also writing a book about the discourse characteristics of the language used in electronic conferences. She is the co-author of *Dialect Clash in America* (Scarecrow, 1977) and the author of *Anthony Burgess: A Bibliography* (Scarecrow, 1980), and she has published essays in journals such as *The SECOL Review, Language in Society, Orbis: Bulletin international de Documentation linguistique,* and *American Speech,* as well as book chapters in several collections about language variation and language use.